INTENTIONAL PRINTING

Simple Techniques for Inspired Fabric Art

LYNN KRAWCZYK

INTERWEAVE.
interweave.com

For my parents, who gave me
everything so I could be anything.

EDITOR Michelle Bredeson

ASSOCIATE ART DIRECTOR Julia Boyles

COVER & INTERIOR DESIGN Adrian Newman

PHOTOGRAPHER Joe Coca

PHOTO STYLIST Ann Swanson

PRODUCTION DESIGNER Katherine Jackson

© 2014 Lynn Krawczyk

Photography and illustrations
© 2014 Interweave

Interweave
A division of F+W Media, Inc.
201 East Fourth Street
Loveland, CO 80537
interweave.com

Manufactured in China
by RR Donnelley Shenzhen.

Library of Congress
Cataloging-in-Publication Data
Krawczyk, Lynn.
Intentional Printing : simple techniques
for inspired fabric art / Lynn Krawczyk.
pages cm
Includes index.

ISBN 978-1-62033-056-2 (pbk)
ISBN 978-1-62033-057-9 (**PDF**)

1. Textile printing. I. Title.
TT852.K73 2014
746.6--dc23
2013032241

10 9 8 7 6 5 4 3 2 1

CONTENTS

INTRODUCTION

Years ago, I was at a crossroads with my fiber art, stuck somewhere between art quilting and an interest in surface design. I was at a loss as to how to meld them into my own style and create original work, so I decided to stop trying. I decided that I would simply experiment and see where it took me.

I created a wide range of oddities: three-dimensional, lopsided fabric bowls, long strips of meticulously handstitched fabric, hideous color combinations of hand-dyed fabric. Nothing had a purpose other than to keep myself working while my creative self solved the riddle of what kind of art I should be making. My studio overflowed with misshapen, unattractive projects.

I began to question everything. "Maybe I'm not an artist," I thought. "Maybe I'm no good." I took one of my less chaotic creations over to a friend's house and lamented over my lack of direction. She became very quiet, then said, "What do you want it to be?" I stared at the tortured fabric object sitting between us. Mostly I wanted it to not be ugly. But in the end, all I could say was, "I have no idea." So I went home and continued to make bad art.

One evening, I sat stewing over the corner I had painted myself into as my friend's question kept rolling around in my mind: "What do you want it to be?" I finally realized there was another side to those seven words I hadn't considered before, one that went far beyond a single project and into the bigger area of my artful self. As soon as the rush

Layered printing (page 92) is an application of intentional printing I use frequently in my work.

of understanding came, a small edge of despair followed. I didn't have an answer. But now I at least understood the question, and that felt like a major step in the right direction.

I came to realize that I had labored under the idea that when I worked in the studio my creative self was in charge. I fretted that if I voiced too strong an opinion, I would stifle the flow of creativity. I finally understood that I was letting my creative self do all the work; I was burdening it with too much expectation. How unfair.

From that moment on, I began to really look at how I made art and ask myself some new questions. What do I like? What don't I like? If no one's opinion but mine counted, what would I make? What habits do I have in the studio that are an asset to my art making? Which ones are sabotaging it?

I began to work alongside my creative self, moving as a team. I stopped being timid and connected with what I was doing. And art became easier, a place without worry or angst. I found that sweet spot in my studio and in my art that had been eluding me for so long.

This book is meant to help guide you toward your own kind of understanding about your art. Yes, there are techniques and there are projects to help you refine your skills. But there is more than that. I can teach you technique until the cows come home, but I'm doing you a disservice if I don't help nudge you toward assimilating these new skills into your personal vision.

Intentional printing is about slowing down and looking beyond the mechanics of how to print pattern on fabric. It's about discovering your intention toward your art by slowing down, getting to know what you love, and embracing the techniques that you learn to create your own art. It's permission to go inward and focus on the aspects of your art that speak your truth the clearest.

Here's to finding your own sweet spot.

INTENTIONAL PRINTING IN ACTION

The easiest way to demonstrate the flexibility of intentional printing is to set it loose among six artists with varying styles. I've chosen five textile artists, in addition to myself, who have very clear visions of the work they create. Their styles are well-defined, and their work is distinctive. Using the principles of intentional printing, I printed fabric that is customized to their styles and asked them to make a project from them. Throughout this book we'll visit with each of the artists and see her approach to working with fabric produced by intentional printing.

CHAPTER 1.

EXPLORING INTENTIONAL PRINTING

Being an artist is about more than the techniques used to create your work. A clear understanding of how you move through your creative practice is just as important. Acting with intention when it comes to your art is about striking a balance between spontaneity and purpose. The combination is powerful and liberating. In this chapter, we'll explore the basic ideas of intentional printing and learn how to harness them in our work.

WHAT IS INTENTIONAL PRINTING?

"What do I do with it now?" This is the eternal question every fiber artist has asked herself when faced with a hunk of handprinted fabric.

When I first began working in surface design, I accumulated a giant pile of printed fabric. After it reached epic heights, I decided to sort it into two piles: pieces that I loved and would use in a project and those that I thought would make great backings for projects. The latter category had the most by a landslide.

That's when I realized I needed to make a change. Making fabric with the hope that it *might* work in a piece of artwork felt like a waste of time and resources. I needed to make fabric *for* a project. And so intentional printing began.

I threw away everything from my art-making process and started rebuilding from the ground up. Two things topped the list of problems I wanted to change. The first was that I was relying too heavily on serendipity in my work, that eternal hope that a bolt of inspiration will strike and I'll create a really stunning piece of art.

The second issue was that I was experimenting too much. I was trapped in a constant cycle of distraction and wanted to try everything new that came down the pipe. I was constantly starting over, never getting good at anything, and my work reflected the unrefined quality that comes with having just learned something.

The goal became clear: to construct a way of working that gave me more control in the art-making process without strangling the creative groove and to pick a facet of surface design that I truly loved and see how far I could push it.

There was a lot of angst and tortured fabric over the course of the year it took to answer these questions. But once I got to the end of it, I discovered something I hadn't expected to: I found my artistic voice.

The following sections lay down the way I created intentional printing. Reading them is a good start, but they are just that—a beginning. Intentional printing is a practice, a way of working that connects you to your artwork through not only skill but emotion as well. It takes time to become comfortable with it, but it's worth it. The best gift you can give yourself as an artist is the understanding that art is not a race. There is no finish line, so there's no point to rushing through. Slow down, find your niche, stay awhile.

Let's begin.

If you create a project with intention, you'll likely be much happier with the results. Even in a project as simple as these Fabric-Wrapped Catchall Boxes (page 120), the colors and prints were carefully thought out.

A LITTLE SELF-AWARENESS

I can give you all the advice in the world about how to print fabric, but the first thing I learned when I set out on my quest to streamline the way I work was that I needed to pay more attention to the way I approached art making. Some of it was good, and some of it? Well, some of it needed to be banished. A little self-awareness will serve you very well in your studio habits.

ARTISTIC PERSONALITIES

I've noticed that there are basically three types of artists. Now, before you start wagging a finger at me and refusing to be classified, hear me out. We are what we are and can't fight our natures, but it doesn't mean we should turn a blind eye to those things that turn the act of making art into something difficult.

Each artistic type has its own set of bad habits. Just being aware of bad habits is often enough to knock them out of the way when they start to rear their ugly heads. Odds are that you are a hybrid of the types listed below (I definitely am), but if you identify the habits that you use to procrastinate in the studio, you'll find a new kind of freedom.

The Ph.D. Artist

The Ph.D. artist needs to know everything. And I mean *everything*. It's not enough to know how to stamp an image onto fabric. She needs to know the chemical composition of the rubber for the stamp, the optimal angle at which the carving tool is held, and the projected life expectancy of the print based on sunlight exposure and care of a particular paint. It's a spectacular show of hoarding information. While gathering knowledge is admirable and necessary, it can turn into a procrastination tool.

Knowing how to do something is one thing. But never putting the information to work renders it useless. If you are a Ph.D. artist, set yourself a time limit for your hunting and gathering. Cut yourself off at some point and start working.

The Flower Child Artist

This is a seriously happy artist. She will try anything anyone puts in front of her. She adores everything she makes and doesn't care about instructions. As long as she is making something, that's good enough. And the more techniques and products the better; there can never be enough to play with in the studio!

Play is important. Too many rules and too much seriousness will dampen anyone's enthusiasm for her art, but it too needs a limit. There isn't enough time in the world to do everything (trust me, I've tried), and so whether we like it or not, we need to narrow our focus a bit. The area you choose to focus on can still be broad, like printing fabric, but when you pull your focus down to a manageable level, the stress that comes with constant experimentation will be gone.

The Worrier Artist

Insecurity reigns supreme with this artist. If it isn't perfect, she believes it isn't worth doing. Every movement she makes is plagued with worry over what others will think or about mistakes that haven't even happened yet. She can't bear the thought of criticism or rejection. The solution? She just doesn't make art at all.

I wish insecurity wasn't part of being an artist, but it is. Angst will sneak up on you when you least expect it. But ask yourself this question: why are you an artist? You can't change other people's opinions, but it doesn't mean your art is no good. It just means it's different from their personal preferences. So check the worry at the studio door, and lose yourself in your art.

PERMISSION TO CHANGE THINGS

It's amazing how we so often cling to a way of doing things that we don't like simply because that's how we were taught to do it. This can apply to anything in the studio, from the way you cut your fabric, to the order of assembly on a project, to the way your studio is arranged.

The way things are shown is not the only way. And that applies to everything in this book as well. While there are certain components that can't be altered, if you want something to work (I haven't found a way to screen print without mesh yet), don't feel you can't tweak things to make them more enjoyable for you.

Think about the elements of your working process that drive you up a wall. Identify the ones that can be changed (unfortunately having your worktable clean itself isn't one of the things that can be on the list) and then *change them*. Your art making is your time. Do it the way you want to.

THE PERFECTION MYTH

I've got a secret for you: there is no such thing as perfection. Doesn't exist. And if you cling to the idea that it does and you can somehow get there, you'll drive yourself mad. It's okay to make mistakes. In fact, it's more than okay—it's necessary. You won't learn about yourself or your art until you screw things up. There's really no other way to say it. Mistakes are the ultimate teacher in everything, especially in art. So fly without a safety net, and know that the world will keep on trucking even if you make a mistake.

THE CREATIVE GROOVE

It may sound like a peculiar dance, but I'm pretty sure you know what I'm talking about. No doubt you've called it by many names—inspiration, serendipity, the flow, your muse, the zone—everyone who is creative recognizes that silent partner that is present during art making.

The creative groove is a partnership between serendipity and intentional decisions on your part. It recognizes that your artistic self has a very particular agenda: it simply wants to create. Nothing more. It doesn't judge if it's good or bad or too blue or kind of crooked. It just wants to spill itself all over, guiding your hands as you work.

While surrendering yourself to that invisible friend is important, you have to bring something to the table. Inspiration isn't enough; you have to stand beside it and make the choices that will take a simple image in your mind's eye and turn it into something tangible.

Making these choices is what we are going to look at next. We're going to learn to tie our choices to our own personal viewpoints so that our creative selves can be free to get lost in the creative groove.

KNOWING WHAT YOU LIKE

I'm convinced that having a strong voice in your art is as simple as knowing what you like. Sound oversimplified? Maybe. But think about your favorite artists. What are the common elements in their artwork? Do they use the same color consistently? Or the same image? Or maybe it's just a style of composition that intrigues you. Odds are that you are attracted to them because *they know what they like,* and there is a consistency in their work. The things that we choose to put in our art are direct reflections of our personalities, and that translates into your artistic voice.

Intentional printing focuses on the two most basic elements of art making: color and imagery. Everything else in a piece gets built up around these two things. We're going to dive into them but from a slightly different angle than you may have encountered before.

COLOR

My Reclaimed Intentions Banner (page 142) began life as an entirely different project that wasn't coming together as I had planned. If a project isn't working for you, don't be afraid to change it or start over.

Color theory is a beast. And while I find it fascinating, I admit that it can get extremely academic very quickly (if you're a Ph.D. artist, no doubt you are thrilled). I could wax poetic at you about the primary and secondary and tertiary colors. We could spend endless time examining hues and tints and saturations.

But we aren't going to. I just want to examine one aspect of color that is sometimes overlooked: how it makes you *feel.*

I've got two questions for you: What's your favorite color? And why? Many times we don't give much thought to why we like something. But maybe we should. Because there is always a deep emotional connection to it, even when it's something as basic as color.

For example, my favorite color is burnt orange. Why? Because I'm a child of the seventies, and the color reminds me of the big orange velvet sofa in the room where I watched television when I was a little girl. I spent many afternoons cuddled in the corner of that couch watching *Mister Rogers' Neighborhood* and *Sesame Street*, surrounded by burnt orange.

The color is comforting, safe, happy. While I may not always use that specific color in every single piece of my work, I gravitate strongly toward earth- and jewel-tone colors. This is probably because they were my first experience with color when I was young, and they conjure up happiness.

Color is the gateway to your art, one of the first things that draws people toward it. You could create a serene landscape full of pastels or a graphic abstract in high-contrast black and white. Either one creates a specific viewing experience.

While the color wheel can help you figure out which colors play nicely together (and we are going to go at least that far into color theory), it's important to spend just as much time thinking about how color makes you feel.

With all this in mind, let's take a quick look at the color wheel. I want you to notice a couple of things about how the colors are placed next to each other.

The colors placed opposite each other have a lot of contrast. This contrast creates a sense of tension when they are placed in the same piece. Tension doesn't necessarily mean a negative response. It can be used to describe excitement, energy, drama. All of these have an underlying tension to them; they are struggling to convey something loud and proud.

The colors placed next to each other are similar to each other; they have lower contrast. Since they are variations of the same color base, they feel calmer, more like friends. They don't work as hard to make you look at them, and that makes them a comfortable place to stop and rest.

This sense of emotion is what I want you to consider when you're choosing which colors to work with. You should always keep in mind that a color you love might make someone else wrinkle their nose in disgust. I have two words about that: *personal preference*. Just because someone else likes something doesn't mean you have to. Use the colors you love.

To further drive home the idea that choosing color is just as much about the color wheel as it is about how it makes us feel, let's do a little exercise. I created the swatches on the opposite page using fabric and paint from my studio. Spend some time looking at them, and jot down how they make you feel.

The next time you begin working on a new project, take a moment to first think about the emotion you want to convey, and then make some color swatches that remind you of that. It's a great way to create a habit of choosing colors with feelings in mind.

My favorite color, burnt orange, and other earth tones make frequent appearances in my artwork, as in these fabric tiles (page 132).

The color wheel is a great base to work from when you're struggling with a color dilemma.

Color Exercise #1

Color Exercise #2

Color Exercise #3

Color Exercise #4

Color Exercise #5

Color Exercise #6

These exercises can help you identify the colors that speak to you. Spend a moment with each swatch and think about how the colors of the paints and the fabrics (and how they relate to each other) make you feel. Make notes you can refer to later when choosing colors for fabric printing.

IMAGERY

Imagery is similar to color. We tend to use the same images over and over again in our work. Whether you are an abstract or representational artist, the idea is the same: focus on the images you love and explore using them in various ways.

I can't tell you the freedom and relief that comes from narrowing your focus. I was paralyzed with too many choices before I realized that was the problem and why my work was all over the place. But once I decided to limit things, I became more relaxed and making art became more fun. Narrowing your focus on the images you use can really help your voice show strongly.

I'm an abstract artist, so I gravitate toward graphic shapes. Circles are a constant favorite of mine; I stick them on everything. And lest you think you're getting off the hook of having to explain yourself when it comes to imagery, think again. Just like color, it's important to know why you like what you are using.

I use circles because they break up the monotony of straight lines and organization. They are energetic and create an easy movement that I wish I had in all areas of my life. They can't be contained easily, yet you can still see what is going on by looking through them. I view them as a looking glass between the structured to-do list of my life and the tug of the freedom I feel when I work in my studio.

Give it some serious thought: why do you use the images you do? There is no right or wrong answer, just awareness. Once you have that, spend some quality time manipulating the different ways you can convey that image.

Let's look at my circles. Yes, they are a basic shape, but how many ways can they be represented? If I put the same size, color, thickness, and shape circle on every piece of artwork I made, I'd create cohesiveness but also a sense of boredom. Varying the shape and viewing it in different configurations creates a thread through my work that becomes a trademark but also keeps things from becoming a snooze fest.

Let's torture this idea a little bit, shall we? Take a look at the swatches on the opposite page and see what happens when I change the size of the circle, the thickness of the line I use to create a circle, and the placement of the circle, whether alone or with its friends.

You see? There is continuity but also interest. There are other shapes that I use consistently; the X, a straight line, and text are all very common elements in my work. So don't feel that you have to tie yourself to one image, but spend some time experimenting with the different ways you can manipulate the images you love.

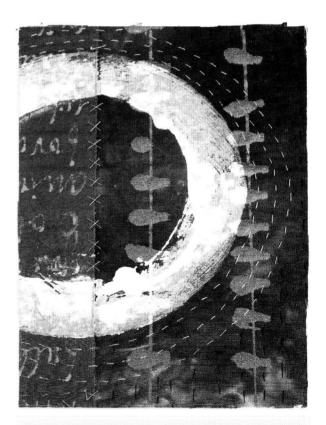

Handstitching around the circle motifs in my Color-Block Table Runner (page 116) further emphasizes their shape. I used two different-size circles for more visual interest.

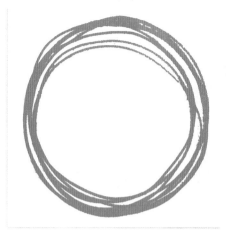

Thin lines lend a sense of fragility to an image.

Heavy, rough printing creates an imposing feeling.

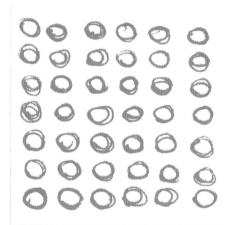

Thin, small-scale groupings work well as background elements because they're easy to overprint with larger-scale images.

Closely spaced patterns can be used to create a focal point in compositions.

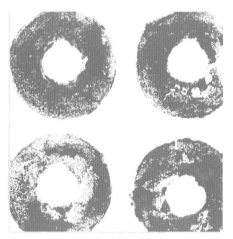

Uneven prints reveal printed layers below. Embrace incomplete shapes as they add interest.

Letting images "hang" off the edge of the fabric creates a sense of movement and the impression that they are moving off into space.

TRANSLATING YOUR AWARENESS INTO ART

Up until this point, we've done a lot of thinking about ourselves. And that's good. It gives us a strong foothold in our own art-making process so that we are no longer tourists on the journey; we are now active participants. We know what colors we like and what images we want to use, and more importantly, we know *why*. That puts us in touch with our creative self by linking emotion with decision making. We're ready to start working.

The remainder of this book is about action. We must now start making the work. After reviewing some basic materials used in the process, we'll learn printing skills, then composition skills through layered printing, and finally we'll put them together by walking through specific project ideas.

The important thing to remember is that art, by its nature, is a challenging process. You turn yourself inside out to get at the idea in your mind and then build yourself back up during its creation. Having intention does not mean you won't face obstacles. It simply means you are willing to face and work through them.

And now it's time to get messy—let's go!

Make swatches to remind yourself of the colors and images that resonate with you. When you're ready to create fabric and artwork, you'll have an invaluable reference to draw from.

THE ALL-IMPORTANT SKETCHBOOK

A sketchbook is your best friend. It's a place to put all the ideas that strike you in odd moments or to work through issues with a project. The biggest thing to remember is that there is no right way to keep a sketchbook.

I have a utilitarian viewpoint when it comes to sketchbooks. I make my sketchbook work. I scribble and sketch and make tons of mistakes.

If there is one thing I think a sketchbook should be, it's a place to make mistakes without regret. It can be filled with watercolor portraits, intricate line drawings, lists of tasks to complete, photos glued in place, or doodles. It all depends on what is inside your head that you want to get out.

HERE ARE A FEW TIPS FOR DEVELOPING A SKETCHBOOK PRACTICE:

★ Have more than one size. It's a good idea to keep a smaller version with you as well as a larger one that can hang about the house.

★ Choose paper that is appropriate to how you want to use the book. Heavier paper will be needed if you want to use paint or markers. Regular writing weight works just fine if you prefer to use only pen or pencil.

★ A sketchbook is not sacred. Experiment. If it bothers you to keep pages around that are a hot mess, tear them out and throw them in the trash. Remember that you are the boss, not the book.

★ Use it as a place for the start of ideas. Don't try to take a project to completion on the pages. Instead, work through the beginning, and let the project evolve as you work on it. Trying to plan every detail destroys spontaneity and can make you feel too restricted.

★ Debate your designs. Write down different options for what you are working on. Sometimes seeing it in writing helps the choice become clear.

There are a lot of ways to keep a sketchbook. I'm hard pressed to tell you that you *have* to do it a certain way. Some like to make their sketchbooks actual pieces of art, while for me that's too much pressure. I need a place that can be somewhat simple. It's a dumping ground for me: the good, the bad, and the ugly all go in there. However you choose to use yours, just make sure it works for you.

My favorite sketchbook contains basic paper, and I always sketch and take notes with a simple pen. I never use color in my sketchbooks; my sketches are kept simple so that my creative side can still have plenty of input when I start working on the actual piece of artwork.

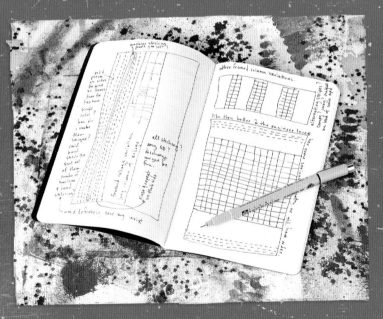

INTENTIONAL PRINTING IN ACTION

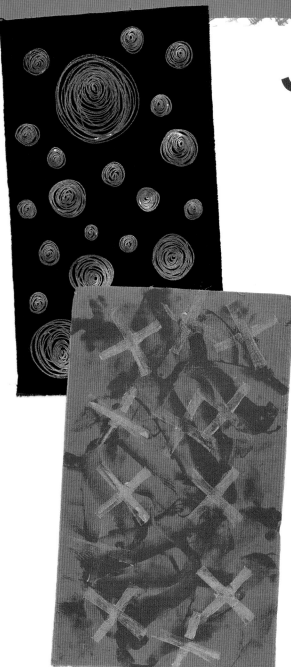

Jamie Fingal

Jamie's style is whimsy defined. Her work is colorful and vibrant, full of attitude, and always playful. The fabric I printed for her played off the jewel tones she often uses as well as her love of polka dots and contrasting colors.

66

Working with the printed fabrics was a bit of a challenge for me because I normally make most of my pieces with commercial cottons and batiks. Also, because the main colors were orange and black, I wanted to avoid anything reminiscent of Halloween. I like a challenge, though, and in keeping with the series that I was working on at the time, I decided to make the orange fabric the background and the black-and-gray polka-dot into a dress that would be the focal point of the piece. To create a fun, full dress, I added a couple of fabrics that were the same value as the black-and-gray fabric from Lynn. They look like they were made to go together.

99

— *Jamie Fingal*

Printing techniques: Top: Drawing on fabric (page 42); bottom: fluid painting (page 46) and stamping (page 52).

OPPOSITE: *Twirly Dress.* 13" × 18" (33 × 45.5 cm); fused appliqué, machine stitching; commercial and handprinted fabrics.

CHAPTER 2

TOOLS & MATERIALS

Setting yourself up for success in fabric printing is as easy as using the right tools and materials, but there are so many options available it can be overwhelming. We artists are fortunate to have so many to pick from! This chapter describes some of my favorite printing tools, paints, and fabrics to help you get started building your toolbox.

PRINTING TOOLS

My interest in printing on fabric grew out of a great admiration for traditional printmaking techniques. There are a lot of aspects of printmaking that won't translate to fabric, so over time I've searched out tools that play well with fiber.

You can use nearly anything to print on fabric. If the paint will stick to it and you can stamp or roll it across the fabric, it's a printing tool. Some are more elegant than others, but don't dismiss something you find interesting simply because it doesn't fit into the traditional category of printmaking tools.

Here are some of the tools that I use all the time in my artwork.

FOAM BRUSHES

Foam brushes are perfect for painting large blocks of color on fabric. Because they are more absorbent than regular brushes, they can create uneven prints when used to paint directly on fabric. I like the rough quality this adds, but you might prefer to use a regular brush for a more even effect. They also work well for virtually every printing technique that requires a tool to push paint through an opening such as a screen or stencil.

RUBBER BRAYER

A brayer is similar to a roller that you would use when painting your walls except there isn't a fuzzy cozy over it. Using a brayer is a simple way to lay paint down quickly.

GELLI ARTS GEL PRINTING PLATE

Monoprinting (a printmaking technique in which a single print is created) often involves a gelatin plate. The Gelli Arts Gel Printing Plate is made of a durable gel that makes monoprinting incredibly convenient and easy. And because it's reusable, it's always ready to go when you are.

PLASTIC STENCILS

Plastic stencils are an easy way to create shapes on fabric. They require a little finesse to get a clean print, but the sometimes-ragged prints they can produce add a nice element to layered work.

PAPIER MÂCHÉ BOX LIDS

The lids from papier mâché boxes are great tools for creating weathered-looking prints. They come in all sizes and shapes, can easily be found in craft stores, and are super-easy on the budget.

THERMOFAX SCREENS

These screens are cousins to the traditional silk screens used for screen printing. The primary difference is that these screens are created using an old photocopy technology—Thermofax machines—eliminating the need for chemicals and a darkroom. Thermofax machines are a bit pricey, but you can also purchase premade screens (see Resources).

MORE HELPFUL TOOLS

Other tools that are useful for printing fabric include eyedroppers, plastic palette knives, plastic scrapers, pool noodles, and homemade foam stamps. The important thing to remember when printing fabric is that if you find something that puts paint down on fabric the way you want it to, it's an excellent tool.

Experiment and you'll find your go-to tools in short order. Having a core group of printing tools, like the ones I've listed above, helps create a more cohesive look to your work because they provide a kind of consistent imagery. Something to think about as you continue to explore the idea of becoming more intentional and focused in your art making.

> **TIP:** *Don't disregard something simply because it seems too simple to use as a printing tool or is a cast-off from another project. Papier mâché lids are one of my favorite printing tools. A lid was heading toward the trash can when I accidentally spilled paint on it. Rather than waste the paint, I pressed it against a piece of fabric, and now those prints show up in nearly all of my work.*

Foam brushes, rubber brayers, eyedroppers, plastic palette knives, the Gelli Arts Gel Printing Plate, and plastic scrapers are handy tools you will use for many printing techniques.

A few of my favorite and more unusual printing tools: papier mâché lids, homemade rubber-foam stamps, Thermofax screens, stencils, and cut-up pool noodles.

FABRIC

Let's talk fabric, shall we? Some surface-design processes, such as dyeing, do require a particular kind of fabric called PFD (Prepared for Dyeing) fabric (it's free of sizing, so the dye can bond with the fibers).

But using paint offers you the freedom to use whatever fabric strikes your fancy. It's an equal-opportunity surface-design medium—it'll stick to almost anything. Feel free to work on whatever you have: commercial or hand-dyed fabric or even secondhand thrift finds.

I'm a cotton girl. That's what I use all of the time without exception. In terms of commercial fabrics, I work with Kaufman Kona cotton the majority of the time. It's a robust fabric that holds up wonderfully to surface design and comes in nearly every color of the rainbow.

But that doesn't mean printing with paint doesn't work on other types of fabric. Use what you love, but be aware that some fabric contents require paint specially formulated to them, and you'll need to follow suit.

Since I use what I have, that often means I work on fabric that already has color on it. When I began printing my own fabric, I worked on white fabric. I quickly tired of having to go back and fill in white gaps that got missed during the printing process, so I began working on fabric that already has color on it.

Working this way has forced me to be more conscious of how colors interact with each other. It's like color mixing directly on the fabric. You can get a lot of different effects depending on the fabric you use. The thing to bear in mind, if you choose to work this way, is the color of the paint shifts on the fabric based on how strong the fabric color is and how strong or weak the opacity of the paint is. In other words, the way the paint color looks in the bottle may not be how it looks when printed on fabric that already has color on it.

If you are making fabric for an item that will see regular washing, prewashing your fabric prior to printing is a good idea. If it's for art that will go on a wall, it's not necessary. I've encountered very few problems with sizing on fabric interfering with paint. I won't say it never happens, but in my experience, it's rare. If you're concerned, give your fabric a spin through the washing machine to be sure.

Kona cotton fabric, my choice for almost all of my projects, comes in a huge array of colors.

PAINT

After an incredible amount of experimentation, paint became my go-to surface-design tool. Here's my top-ten list of reasons why I prefer paint more than any other medium:

1. It's readily available in stores and online.

2. Any acrylic paint can be transformed into textile paint by adding textile medium to it.

3. Making it permanent is as simple as ironing it.

4. It doesn't break the bank.

5. The results are consistent; there is very little variation.

6. There's no prep work involved; open the jar and get to work.

7. No toxic chemicals are needed.

8. No special fabric is required.

9. It can be applied in endless ways: screen it, stamp it, brush it, brayer it.

10. It comes in a wide variety of colors and finishes.

With so many paints available, the choices can be overwhelming. These are my go-to paints and inks for fabric printing.

All paint consists of two things: a binder (the liquid part) and pigment (the color part). The most common type of textile paint you will use is acrylic paint. Acrylic paint is a fascinating fellow; it's basically a plastic binder with color trapped inside it. It might sound weird that you're putting plastic on your fabric, but its versatility makes it a rock star. You can mix it with a variety of mediums to make it do your bidding, and often you can mix brands for new colors, since acrylics share the same characteristics.

Paint is not the same as dye. It sits on top of the fabric rather than bonding with the fibers like dye does. As a result, you'll notice a change in the hand of the fabric. Textile paint is formulated to reduce this effect, but it's good to keep in mind that fabric printed with paint will never be as soft as fabric printed with dye. You can still stitch through it and wash it and wear it, but it's important to note.

This section is going to give you a good feel for how paint behaves and what kind you should use on your fabric projects. It's important to find the paint that you love best; it's a little bit like dating—you just won't know if you love it until you spend some time with it. It's easy to get swept away with enthusiasm and buy twenty bottles of a brand (ask me how I know), but dig deep and restrain yourself until you find one that you think is groovy. You'll be happy you did some trials before stocking your cupboards.

OPACITY, VISCOSITY & FINISH

When we talk about paint, we'll be using a set of terms that are helpful to understand.

Opacity

This refers to whether the paint produces a see-through print or a solid print. Low-opacity paint will allow the colors beneath it to show through. High-opacity paint completely covers whatever is beneath it. Metallic paints will always have a higher opacity due to the addition of the metallic components. This makes them excellent candidates for printing on dark fabric. It's important to note, however, that metallic paints will make your fabrics much stiffer due to the way they are formulated.

I painted a sample piece of fabric showing the concept of opacity. High-opacity paint shows up well on the black fabric, while low-opacity paint does not. From top to bottom, these are the colors I used: Jacquard Neopaque Turquoise, Jacquard Lumiere Metallic Bronze, Jacquard Textile Color Maroon, and Jacquard Neopaque Gold Yellow.

Viscosity

Viscosity refers to how thick the paint is. High viscosity means it's very thick, like Marshmallow Fluff, and low viscosity means it's very thin, like water. Most textile paint falls in the middle of that scale. High- to medium-viscosity paints will produce solid-to semi-solid prints, depending on their opacity. Low-viscosity paints seep into the fabric and behave like watercolor paint and dye.

HIGH- TO MEDIUM-VISCOSITY PAINTS

Jacquard is my go-to paint brand. They have a wide range of colors and opacities. Their Textile Color line produces semi-opaque prints, which work wonderfully for layered printing. Their Neopaque line caters to the need for a good, strong solid print with nothing showing in the background. Their Lumiere line covers all the bases of metallics, giving you a wide range of choices.

LOW-VISCOSITY PAINTS

Once again, I use Jacquard brand here. Their Dye-Na-Flow is an excellent low-viscosity paint. It mimics the intense color of dye in a paint form. It's as fluid as water and creates really beautiful prints on fabric.

Finish

This refers to how the paint looks after it's dry. Matte means there is no shine, semi-gloss means there is a slight shine, and glossy means it's super shiny. Textile paint doesn't often create a glossy finish, but metallic paints have a sheen that pushes them toward that end of the scale.

Paint can also have different finishes: matte (not shiny) or shiny. You can see the difference in the sample I painted with Neopaque paint and metallic paint. The sample on the left is Jacquard Neopaque Green (matte) and the one on the right is Lumiere Metallic Olive Green (shiny).

TEXTILE PAINT VS. NON-TEXTILE PAINT

Textile paint is formulated for use on fabric. It has textile medium in it, which means it helps reduce the chance that it will make the fabric as stiff as a board. Odds are that you will always notice a change in the hand of the fabric when you use paint to print on it, but textile medium greatly reduces this effect.

Now don't turn your back on paint that isn't labeled as being usable on fabric. If you are doing work that will hang on a wall and aren't concerned with the stiffness of the fabric, use whatever paint you like. Bear in mind that it will make stitching difficult, though.

You can also add textile medium to non-textile paint. It's rather fluid, so it will make your paint thinner, but it's a good solution for using the paints you love on fabric.

SPECIALTY PAINTS

Sometimes a printing process will require a specially formulated paint or ink. Screen printing is an example. The thing that makes screen-printing paint special is the drying time; it stays wet much longer than other acrylic paint. This is important because if the paint dries too quickly on your silk screen, it will clog the mesh. That will make future printing with the screen difficult or impossible.

To make sure your screen sticks around for a long time, use paint or ink intended specifically for screen printing. My favorites are Simply Screen screen-printing paint and Versatex screen-printing ink.

CHOOSING COLORS

What colors should you buy? Easy: the ones you love. If you are inclined to color mixing, you can buy just the primary colors (red, yellow, and blue) and take the time to mix every hue under the sun. Or you can buy premixed colors that suit your needs. I'm a firm believer in making things easy, so if you find it simpler to buy premixed colors, go right ahead!

I printed the fabric for the Coffee Talk Hoops (page 112) with textile paints.

good opacity!
decent opacity for a "yellow"
Jacquard Neoopaque 581 Gold Yellow
love the tip on the bottle
good opacity for layering
Plaid Simply Screen Blue Hawaii 98514
LOVE the color but its tone makes it completely opaque. No transparency at all.
Pro chemical & dye Transparent PROfab Indigo 403
not fabric paint
bought @ scrapbook store
but misting effect is interesting & might work well in layers.
mister huey's color mist Leaf green
GREAT opacity!
Jacquard Lumiere 565 Metallic Bronze
AWESOME COLOR!
color shifts closer to a greenish gold when painted on colored fabric
maintains green tone on white
Jacquard Lumiere 562 Metallic Olive Green
reads VERY bright on white. Not too loud over other colors but extremely loud color so needs to be used sparingly.
like it on pale grey, good punch
Jacquard Dye-na-Flow 805 Scarlet
really good semi-opaque
nice purple
totally acts as a transparent, couldn't cover the metallic blue printed circles or brown fabric
Jacquard Textile Color 125 Periwinkle
reads super dark on other colors

CREATING A PAINT DIARY

Since I use paint almost exclusively, I like to keep track of my favorite colors and make notes on how different paints will act on fabric. So I created what I call a "paint diary" that hangs on a studio wall.

My paint diary is actually a canvas runner that I purchased from a home-decorating store and painted with white gesso on each side. You could also use white canvas (no gesso necessary) or just plain white fabric. If you don't like the idea of hanging it on the wall, cut it into small squares to create swatches.

I always include several swatches of each paint in my paint diary. It shows how the color looks on white (painted directly on the canvas) and how it looks on several small squares of colored fabric. This lets me check the paint's opacity and see how it will behave when it's applied to different colors.

The colored fabric squares are glued down to the canvas with my notes written beneath them as needed. It's also a good way to keep track of fabric types and colors that I love.

I'm not obsessive about doing this with every paint that comes through the studio door. You can see that the fabric colors vary, so even that is not consistent. There are even some commercial prints in there. It's just a visual reference that helps me find my place if I'm hemming and hawing about what kind of paint to use on a project.

A paint diary is a handy source of information and inspiration.

SETTING UP A WORK SPACE

As artists we're determined to create and we'll do it anywhere we can. Whether you have a permanent work space or you're a nomad who creates wherever you can find a clean corner to set up shop, there are a few elements to your work space that will make printing fabric easier.

THE PRINT SURFACE

Printing fabric is messy business, which is one of my favorite parts. But the reality of it is that your house and family members most likely won't share your enthusiasm for being covered in paint splotches. (I accidentally painted the dog once; there were several complaints.)

That makes setting up a printing surface a necessity. Luckily, it's a rather easy task that can be made into a permanent fixture in your studio or portable to make cleanup easy if you do your work at the dining room table.

A printing surface consists of three layers: plastic, felt, and canvas. Each layer provides a level of protection that works to keep your house paint-free and avoid printing ghost images on your fabric. The size that you make each layer largely depends on your work space. The most important thing is to avoid seams in the felt and canvas layers because those will show up when you print the fabric laid over top of them. Let's take a quick look at each layer.

Plastic

This layer goes down first and will stop the paint from getting on your table. Plastic painting tarps or plastic trash bags work great. Even if you don't mind if paint gets on your table, still put this layer down. Any wet paint that is hanging around when you are printing can end up on the fabric you're working on, and that's not something you can undo.

Felt

Felt provides some cushion for the printing process. Acrylic craft felt on the bolt works great. If you can't find felt that is large enough for your needs, low-loft batting also works.

Canvas

This is the top layer of your print surface. Its purpose is to catch any paint that makes it through the fabric you are printing. By having fabric as this layer, the paint gets absorbed quickly, and there is less chance of creating unwanted prints on the fabric you are making.

I prefer heavier fabric like canvas because it lasts longer. You can normally find it in the utility fabric section of fabric stores on the bolt. If you use thinner fabric, lay down more than one layer. Also give this layer an iron to get out any folds that might make for bumpy printing.

Cut each layer as big as you need for your work space. It's a good idea to make the plastic layer the largest one so that it creates a kind of plastic "edge" around the other layers. You can use that edge to set down paintbrushes and paint bottles without worrying about stray paint marks.

I find that the layers don't move around when I'm printing. But if you are worried about them shifting, tape the edges down with some duct tape, and you'll be good to go.

Over time, the extra paint that gets absorbed into the print surface creates a really wonderful layered fabric. So hang on to it; it's a great addition to projects.

Permanent vs. Temporary

Depending on your home studio space allocation, you may need to make your printing surface mobile. Mobile print surfaces are also great when you are going to a class or retreat since you can just roll it up and take it with you. I have both types.

My permanent printing table is a fabric-cutting table from a craft store. It is on wheels and has collapsible sides, so I can drag it around my studio at will and change the size as I need it.

A mobile printing surface is simply the three layers we talked about on a small scale. My layers are normally about one yard (1 m) each. It's big enough that it will protect the surface I'm working on but not so large that I can't roll the bugger up and drag it around with me.

DRYING FABRIC

While paint dries relatively quickly, it still needs time to sit undisturbed. This means you'll need some kind of solution for where to put the drying fabric so that it doesn't hog your print table and prevent you from continuing on with another piece of fabric.

There are a couple of solutions for handling the dilemma of drying fabric. If your work space is large enough, set up an extra table or two. Lay plastic over the top of the table and on the ground beneath it so that you can lay wet fabric on both. You can also use collapsible clothes drying racks if you need to be able to put the drying surfaces away when you're done.

A second suggestion is to hang the fabric to dry. Hangers for pants that have grippers work wonderfully for suspending fabric while it dries. Be careful where you hang the fabric, though, so the print doesn't smear or transfer paint to surrounding walls. I like to hang my fabric from the shower curtain rod in my bathroom so it's out of the way. I always scoot the shower curtain to the far end of the rod when I do this. And if the fabric is especially wet and may drip, I'll put plastic down over the edge of the tub and floor to avoid making a huge mess.

While fans may seem like a fantastic idea to speed up the drying process, be careful. If the fabric is not weighted down, it will flop around, and you'll end up with smeared prints.

It's always a good idea to let the fabric dry completely before you move on to the next step of printing or creating a project. It's a little bit of torture but worth it.

CREATING A DESIGN WALL

Design walls are handy tools to use as you're working on a project. Nothing lets you know better if you're on the right track than simply stepping back and assessing something from a few feet away. It also gives you a place to leave a problem project so you can dwell on the solution without it constantly being in the way.

Unfortunately, not all of us have large studios. Mine is modest in size, and while it works for my needs, wall space is limited. My solution to a design wall is a little less glamorous but still functional.

Pink Styrofoam insulation from the home improvement store and white flannel fabric make a quick and easy design board. Cut the Styrofoam to the size your space can accommodate, and then wrap the fabric around it like it's a present. Secure it on the back with pins or duct tape. You can attach it to a wall (mine is held up with Velcro strips) or leave it freestanding to move around your space as needed.

Don't hang wet fabric on your design board to dry; it will most likely leave paint marks on the fabric you used to create the board.

If you absolutely do not have the space to create a design wall, don't fret. Find a place where you can tack your project up periodically and step back to study it. You'll find that it takes on a different appearance when it's hanging a few feet away than when you are staring at it on your print table. That change in perspective is essential for catching things you don't like or deciding what to do next.

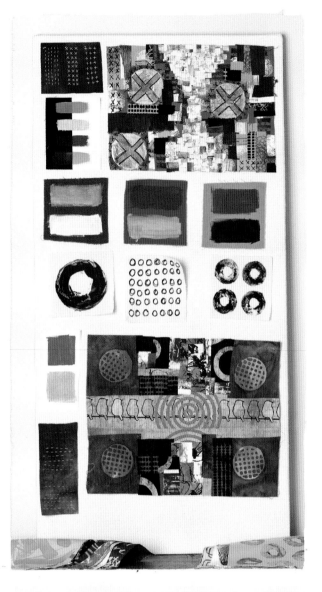

A design wall is ideal for trying out ideas and getting a fresh perspective on your work.

WORK SPACE SAFETY

Luckily, working with paint doesn't pose too many safety risks. But there are a few things you should keep in mind to maintain a healthy studio environment.

Some paints have a strong odor to them. Unfortunately, you won't really know which ones you find stinky until you try them, but it's always a good idea to work in an area that has windows for fresh air.

If you have sensitive skin, wear latex gloves when you work with paint. It's unavoidable that you'll get paint on yourself when you work, and if you're concerned about annoying your hands, gloves are a good bet.

Acrylic paint does not wash out. Period. So if you're worried about paint on your clothes, dedicate a shirt and pants to your studio work sessions, or invest in an apron that can take the abuse for you. Also, don't work in areas where there is expensive carpet beneath your feet. Paint has a tendency to fling far when you least expect it, so it's best to be cautious.

TIP: Being near a water source is a necessity for working with paint. If you don't have one close by your work area, you can create a temporary one by using a plastic kitty-litter tray filled about one-third full of water. Washing your tools out before the paint has a chance to dry on them will extend their life span.

HAND-DYED FABRIC

Using dye to develop your own palette of fabric to work with is truly one of the best ways to help pull your voice into your work. Hand-dyeing fabric is a broad topic, one this book doesn't cover, as there are many others that do it so well.

I'm not a dyer; I'm a painter (if you hadn't noticed), so I tend to buy my hand-dyed fabric from dyeing artisans. It's quite a labor-intensive process, and while well worth the effort, it's something I like to leave to the experts. (See the Resources section for some of my favorites.)

But if you're thinking about giving it a go, here is some basic information to get you started:

★ Only use fabric that is intended for dyeing. This fabric is called PFD, or Prepared for Dyeing. It is free of any sizing or other additions that would prevent the dye from bonding with the fabric.

★ Any tools that you use for dyeing need to be dedicated to only that activity. Dyeing involves the use of chemicals and powders that should never be consumed. Thrift shops and dollar stores are a good way to build up your tool chest.

★ Invest in a good-quality dust mask. Breathing in dye powders is unhealthy and should be avoided. Working in a well-ventilated area also helps.

★ Using a scale to measure out how much dye powder to use will give you more accurate repeatability than measuring spoons.

★ Keep notes as you work so you can re-create a color if you fall in love with it. A simple notebook works very well.

★ Use dyes that are formulated to the fiber content of the fabric you are working with. Cotton dyes are different from silk dyes. The processes may also differ, so be sure to do your research.

If you want to become a dyeing addict, see the Resources section for recommended reading. In addition to books, there are many online groups and resources to peruse for actual human support. A quick Internet search will turn up many to choose from.

INTENTIONAL PRINTING IN ACTION

Printing technique: Stamping (page 52)

Jenny Doh

Jenny's work is very serene. She has a minimalist style that works to throw the message of her work into sharp relief. It was important to me to keep the fabric design I printed for her clean. Sometimes there is great power in simplicity.

"

I love gray, and so I loved that the fabric was gray with a very minimal design in white. It inspired me to keep things simple. The round motif on the fabric got me in the mood to use circles, along with vertical and horizontal rectangles.

I approached the composition in much the same way that I would create a mixed-media piece. I started by cutting the circles, standing back, then adding the rectangles, stepping back, and then just kept going back and forth with more circles, more lines, and more rectangles. I think with minimalist design composition, it's all about balance. You don't have to have a lot of elements on a piece, but they do have to be arranged so that things feel balanced.

— *Jenny Doh*

"

OPPOSITE: *Love.* 18½" × 22" (47 × 56 cm); raw-edge appliqué, free-motion machine stitching; commercial and handprinted fabrics.

CHAPTER 3

FABRIC-PRINTING TECHNIQUES

In this chapter, we'll learn eight techniques with variations for creating prints on fabric. These printing techniques might seem simple but don't be deceived. Their simplicity is a gateway to creating more complex work: learn each element and you'll be able to combine them effectively whenever you want to.

COLOR-WASH PRINTING

Watercolor paintings are a huge inspiration to me because of the many layers that are needed to create a solid layer of imagery. Something always seems to be hiding just beneath the surface. Color-wash printing creates a similar effect that can be used as a base layer or to obscure images you've already printed.

YOU WILL NEED
- Plastic spoon
- Paint
- Gelli Arts Gel Printing Plate
- Rubber brayer
- Fabric

1. Place a spoonful of paint onto the printing plate (*fig. 1*). Touch the brayer to the edge of it, and roll the brayer back and forth on a part of the plate without paint to create a thin layer of paint across the surface of the brayer (*fig. 2*).

2. Roll the brayer across the fabric in random patterns, letting the fabric wrinkle and shift as you go (*fig. 3*). This creates awesome texture.

3. Repeat Step 1 to reload the brayer with paint, and continue to roll across the fabric until you're happy with the amount of color added (*fig. 4*).

TIPS FOR COLOR-WASH PRINTING

★ The point of this kind of printing isn't to create solid prints. You want the paint to be almost transparent, so go easy on the amount of paint you apply to the fabric.

★ I prefer a rubber brayer more than a hard plastic one because paint sticks better to the rubber.

★ Always wash off your brayer when you're finished. If the paint dries, it can be very difficult to remove and sometimes becomes permanent.

★ If you're printing over top of other printing, make sure the base prints are dry before you apply the color-wash technique.

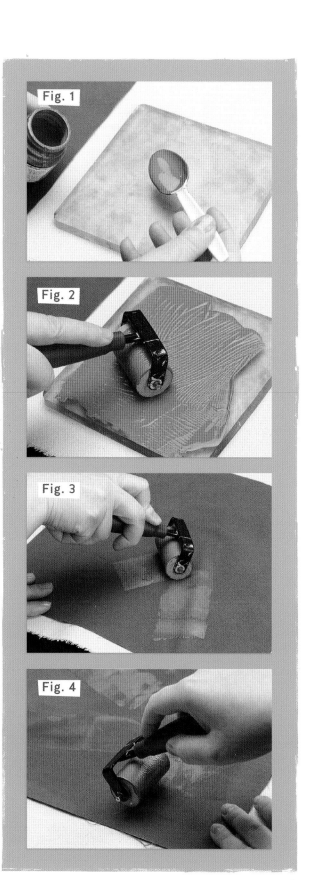

Fig. 1

Fig. 2

Fig. 3

Fig. 4

DRAWING ON FABRIC

We all doodle, whether during meetings, while talking on the phone, or to occupy our time while we're waiting for an appointment. It's a very intuitive process, one that is soothing and familiar. It's easy to doodle on fabric as well. All you need is a bottle with a tip on it to act as your pen, and you're ready to go!

YOU WILL NEED
- Medium-viscosity paint
- Squeeze bottle with tip (I use 2-ounce squeeze bottles from Dick Blick; they are easy to squeeze and hold a good amount of paint.)
- Fabric

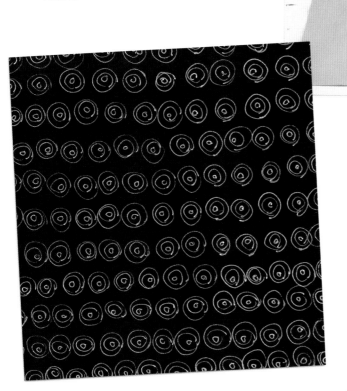

1. Fill your paint bottle halfway with the paint you'd like to draw with.

2. On a scrap piece of fabric, draw a couple of test lines to make sure there isn't any air in the tip. Trapped air will cause splatters and interrupted drawing.

3. Place the tip of the bottle against the fabric with gentle pressure and begin drawing your design. Keep consistent pressure on the bottle so that air can't sneak into the bottle. **Do not** lift the tip off the fabric. Just continue drawing until you reach a breaking point in the design *(figs. 1–3)*.

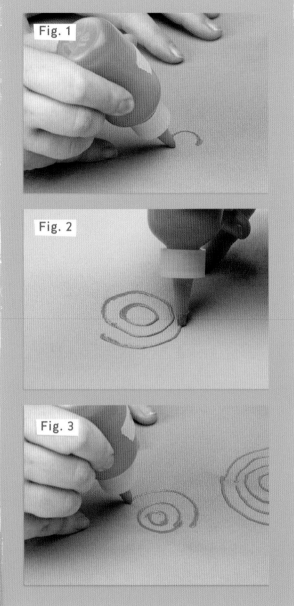

Fig. 1

Fig. 2

Fig. 3

TIPS FOR DRAWING ON FABRIC

★ If you're concerned about fabric moving, you can pin it to your print surface, pulling it slightly so it's taut. You might need to add an extra layer or two to your surface to be able to pin into it.

★ Don't use thick (high-viscosity) paint with this technique. It will leave blobs on the surface of the fabric that can crack or flake off.

★ You might get a little blob at the beginning of each line. Don't get stressed about this; it's part of the "by hand" look we're going for and adds to the charm of your work.

★ Don't store unused paint in the squeeze bottles; the seals are not as secure as on the jars the paint comes in, and the paint could dry out. Squeeze any leftover paint back into the paint jar.

★ Wash out the tips of the bottles when you're done working with them. Dry paint will clog them and be difficult to clean out.

★ If you're writing text, don't worry about what it says or if it's legible. Text creates movement, and there's something very intriguing about adding writing that can't be read to your work.

★ Don't press hard on the fabric with the bottle tip. Too much pressure will cause breaks in the paint line and make the drawing/writing look messy.

FLUID PRINTING

Even though paint is my go-to material for fabric printing, sometimes it's nice to use something more fluid. Luckily for us, we don't have to abandon paint. Dye-Na-Flow paint is completely fluid and has tons of pigment. It creates the richness of dyes without all the mess and fuss of extra chemicals.

I like to use Dye-Na-Flow two different ways: swipe painting and splatter painting. While they may not look that impressive on their own, they work wonderfully in layered printing (see page 92).

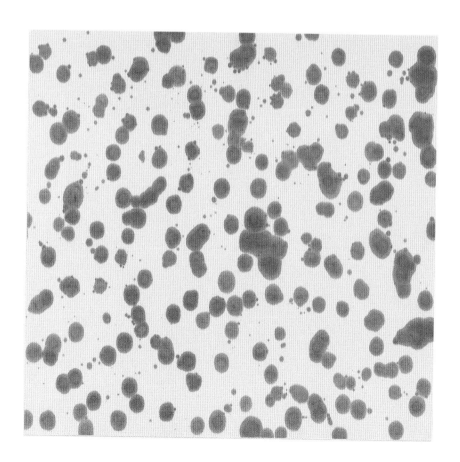

SPLATTER PAINTING

Splatter painting is just what it sounds like—dripping fluid paint and letting it go "splat!" of its own free will. This technique creates a very organic type of pattern because it's impossible to control what the paint will do once it leaves the pipette.

YOU WILL NEED
- Dye-Na-Flow paint
- Paint pipette
- Fabric

1. Fill a paint pipette with fluid paint *(fig. 1)*.

2. Drip the paint over the fabric, letting it splatter randomly in little pools *(figs. 2–4)*.

Fig. 1

Fig. 2

Fig. 3

Fig. 4

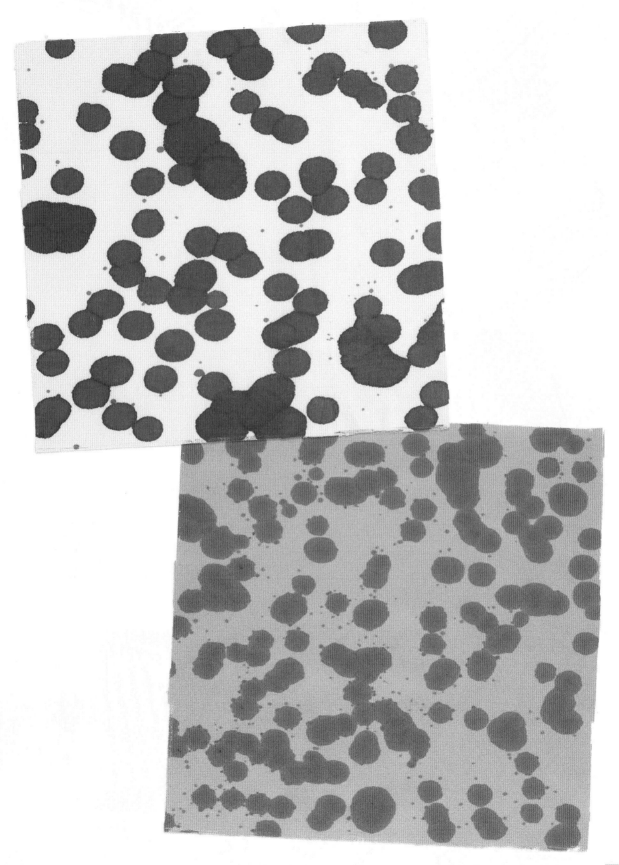

SWIPE PAINTING

Swipe painting is a somewhat controlled way of painting with fluid paint. Because the fluid paint is being moved quickly across the fabric, it holds its shape better than with splatter painting.

YOU WILL NEED
- Dye-Na-Flow paint
- Foam brush
- Fabric

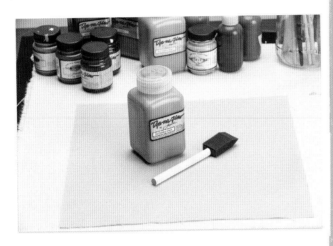

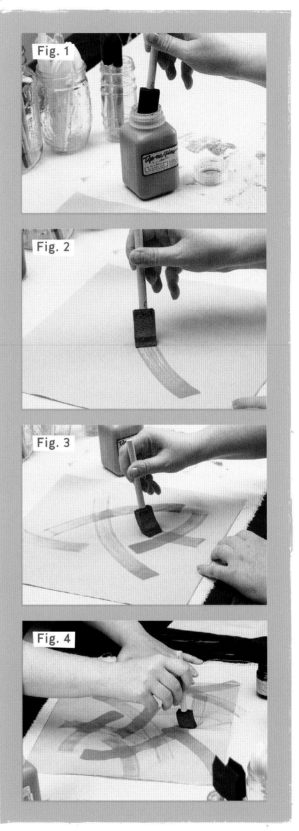

Fig. 1

Fig. 2

Fig. 3

Fig. 4

1. Dip the foam brush into the paint container or pour a small amount of paint into a plastic cup and dip a foam brush into it *(fig. 1)*.

2. Swipe the foam brush across the fabric quickly, creating random patterns *(figs. 2–4)*.

3. You can also just pounce the foam brush tip on the fabric to create random rectangular shapes.

TIPS FOR FLUID PAINTING

★ I use the paint straight out of the bottle to get the richest color. If you'd like a more subtle watercolor effect, experiment with adding different amounts of water to some paint in a cup to get the desired shade.

★ I like to work on dry fabric, but you can work on wet fabric as well. The final pattern will have more of a blurred effect.

★ Because fluid paint is not as stubborn as acrylic paint, it's especially important to set it. You can set fluid paint into the fabric in one of two ways: ironing it after it dries or allowing the fabric to sit for one to two weeks.

STAMPING

There are plenty of ways to create your own stamps. The majority of the ones I've made in the past used pink carving rubber and either a craft knife or carving tools. Unfortunately, I'm a bit of a klutz, and I've cut myself several times. My friend and fellow artist Judi Hurwitt introduced me to a method of stamp making using cardboard and self-adhesive foam sheets. It's flexible and extremely affordable. For little cost, you can experiment and really make them your own.

YOU WILL NEED
- Self-adhesive foam sheets
- Scissors
- Cardboard
- Paint
- Foam brush or rubber brayer
- Fabric

1. Draw or freehand cut your shapes from the self-adhesive foam sheet *(fig. 1)*.

2. Cut a piece of cardboard to the size you want your stamp to be, and stick the foam pieces to it *(figs. 2 and 3)*.

3. Brush paint across the foam with a foam brush *(fig. 4)*.

4. Turn the stamp over and press it onto the fabric *(figs. 5 and 6)*.

5. Lift the stamp up to reveal your print *(fig. 7)*.

6. Repeat Steps 3 through 5 to continue printing the entire surface of the fabric *(fig. 8)*.

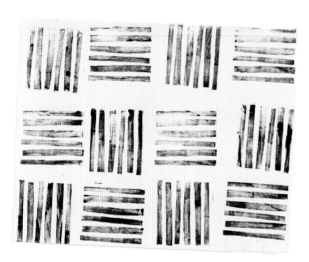

Fig. 1

Fig. 2

Fig. 3

Fig. 4

Fig. 5

Fig. 6

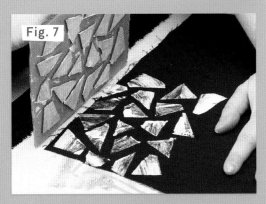
Fig. 7

Fig. 8

TIPS FOR STAMPING

★ If you're creating stamps of letters or numbers, remember to draw or freehand cut them backward so they stamp correctly.

★ If you're printing for a specific project and want to create repeats, size the cardboard to the area you're printing, then arrange the foam pieces in the pattern you want to stamp. (This won't work for a very large piece because the paint will dry before you can cover the entire stamp.)

★ The paint will soak into the foam pieces a little bit the first couple of times you use them. If you want to try to prevent this, you can paint gesso over the foam pieces to seal them. I find gesso's smell to be an irritant (it gives me headaches), plus it's an added expense, so I let the paint layers build up to seal the foam. Honestly, it takes only two or three uses for the paint to stop absorbing into the foam.

★ Using a foam brush causes the brush marks to show on the final stamped image. I appreciate this extra texture, so it doesn't bother me. If you'd like a more even appearance, you can use a rubber brayer to apply the paint to the stamp. This method takes a little more paint.

★ These stamps won't last forever. You can clean them off with baby wipes, but I like to let the paint layers build up.

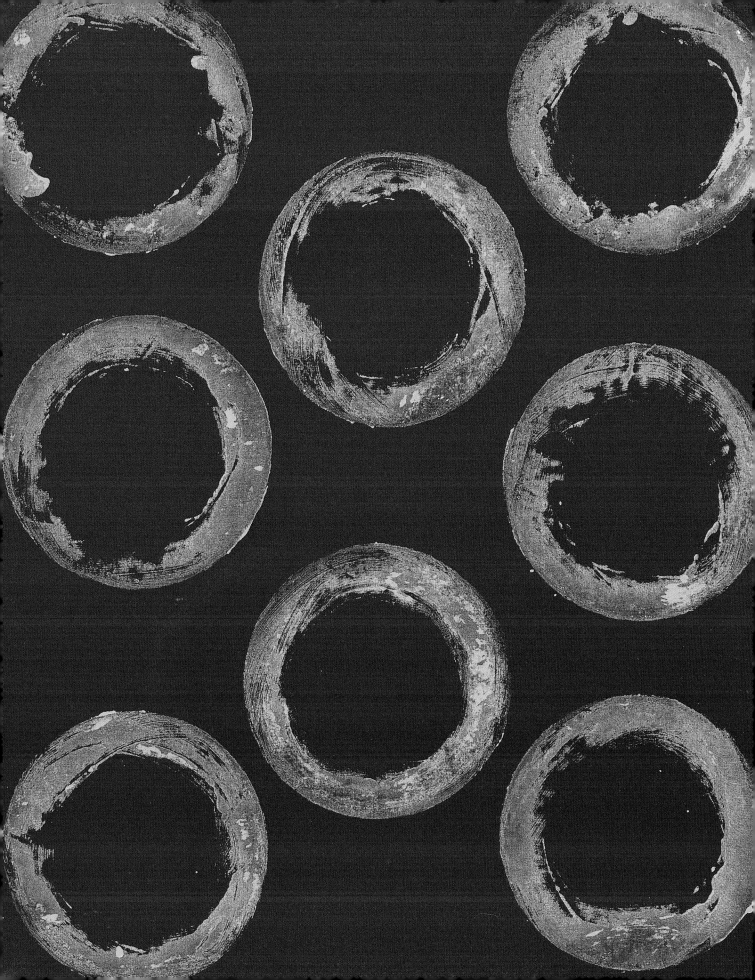

DECAY PRINTING

Decay printing is a term I use for a particular kind of printing that uses found objects. "Found objects" can be anything you wouldn't ordinarily think of using to print on fabric. My favorites are the round lids from papier mâché boxes, foam pool noodles, and plastic letter stencils. The element that ties them all together is that they create imperfect prints. They show what looks like wear or age, which is why I call it decay printing. It reminds me of peeling paint on the side of a building or the scratches that show up on a sign after years of use.

We're going to look at printing with the three found objects I listed above, but don't limit yourself to just those. The sky is the limit.

DECAY PRINTING WITH PAPIER MÂCHÉ LIDS

These prints show up in a lot of my work. Because the lids are porous, you'll eventually need to toss them, but you can get a lot of prints out of them before you get to that point. A key to printing with these lids is to let the paint build up. In other words, don't clean them off. Eventually, the layers will pull off, and you'll get a really nice weathered look to the print.

I have two ways of printing with these lids.

Method 1: Brush on Paint

YOU WILL NEED
- Paint
- Papier mâché lids
- Foam brush
- Fabric

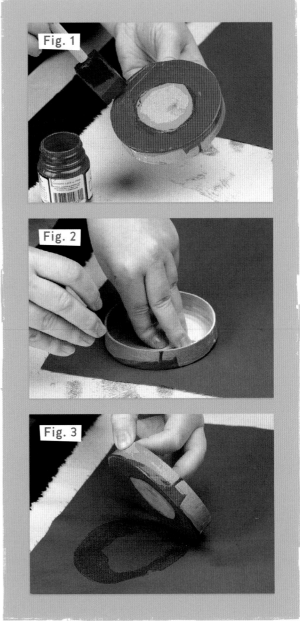

1. Using a foam brush, brush a generous amount of paint around the edge of the lid *(fig. 1)*.

2. Flip the lid over and press it firmly against the fabric *(fig. 2)*.

3. Lift up the lid and check your print *(fig. 3)*.

4. Repeat Steps 1 through 3 to continue printing across the fabric *(figs. 4 and 5)*.

5. Set the lid aside and allow the paint to dry.

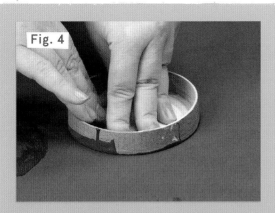

Fig. 4

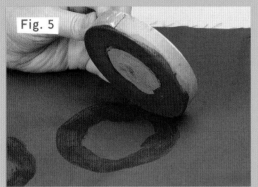

Fig. 5

Method 2: Draw on Paint

1. Pour some paint into a bottle with an applicator tip and draw around the edges of the lid several times, letting the lines overlap and blur into each other.

2. Flip the lid over and press it firmly against the fabric.

3. Lift up the lid, and you're done! If you'd like to continue printing, you will need to add more paint to the lid.

4. Set the lid aside and allow paint to dry.

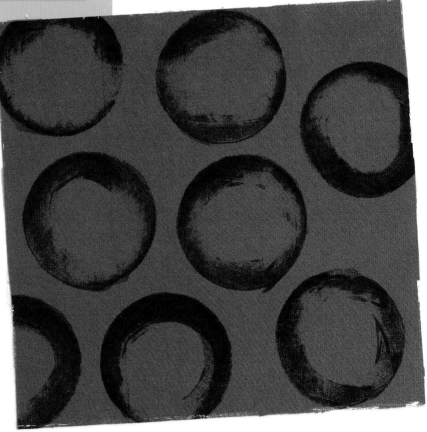

DECAY PRINTING WITH FOAM POOL NOODLES

These odd little foam tubes are used for keeping yourself afloat in a pool, but fiber artists have found other uses for them, including wrapping finished quilts around them for shipping work to shows. I always have a small piece left after wrapping my quilts and decided that if it's taking up space, it's going to earn its keep. Turns out, they make very interesting prints!

YOU WILL NEED
o Paint
o Foam pool noodles cut into short pieces
o Foam brush
o Fabric

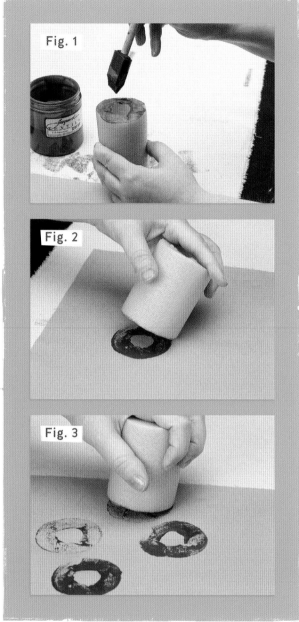

Fig. 1

Fig. 2

Fig. 3

1. Brush a generous amount of paint onto one end of the foam noodle *(fig. 1)*. Don't worry if your cut is uneven; mine always are, and I find it makes the print more interesting.

2. Press the noodle firmly onto the fabric.

3. Lift up the noodle to reveal your print *(fig. 2)*.

4. Follow Steps 2 and 3 to make additional prints *(fig. 3)*. These noodles act a little bit like a sponge, so you can usually print more than one circle with a single application of paint, but they do get lighter with each stamping.

5. Wash the paint off the pool noodle.

DECAY PRINTING WITH PLASTIC LETTER STENCILS

Stencils might not fit your idea of a found object, but I tend to use stencils individually, concentrating on the shape and movement that the letter provides as opposed to the actual letter. Rarely do I spell out a word when I stencil letters; I just enjoy the graphic impact that text provides.

I put stencils in the decay-printing category because they often come out kind of sloppy. I don't worry about paint that slips beneath the stencil and causes uneven lines along the edge of the letter. Again, it reminds me of weathered signs and the way the text degrades over time.

YOU WILL NEED
- Paint
- Plastic letter stencils
- Foam brush
- Fabric

Fig. 1

Fig. 2

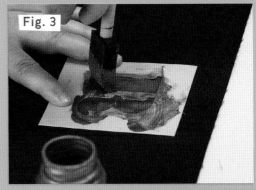

Fig. 3

Fig. 4

1. Dip your foam brush into the paint and dab it onto the closed part of the stencil *(fig. 1)*. This will act as your well to pick up more paint when you need it.

2. Hold the stencil down with one hand and brush the paint in the opening *(figs. 2 and 3)*.

3. Carefully lift the stencil when you're done *(fig. 4)*.

4. Repeat Steps 2 and 3 to create additional prints.

TIPS FOR DECAY PRINTING

★ If you find that you love the shape of a found object but the paint doesn't want to stick to it, try giving the surface a very light sanding to rough it up. That usually does the trick.

★ Some of the paint will remain embedded in the foam pool noodles, but since they're designed to be used in water, you can give them a good scrub.

★ Experiment with different stencil patterns. Consider printing the letters upside down, backward, or close together. Concentrate on the shape and see what emerges.

★ Plastic stencils are more of an investment than their cardboard cousins, but they last forever and can be easily cleaned with warm water and a sponge.

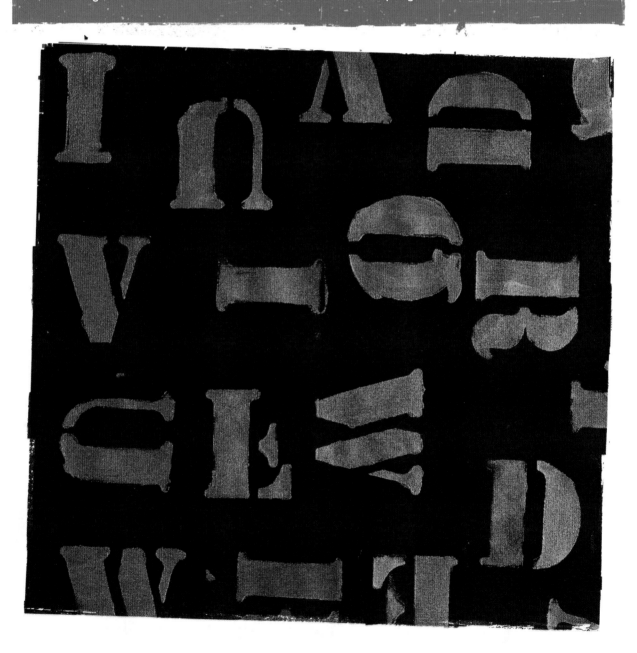

DROP-CLOTH PRINTING

When we talked about setting up a work space, I mentioned the cool random patterns you can get on the fabric that makes up the top layer of your print surface. Well, I'm an impatient artist, so I decided to print fabric that looks like it's been sitting on a print table for ages, picking up leftover paint.

YOU WILL NEED
- Paint (2 or 3 colors)
- Gelli Arts Gel Printing Plate
- Plastic spoons
- Plastic palette knife
- Fabric

This technique uses a Gelli Arts Gel Printing Plate, a reusable plate that acts like the homemade gelatin plate often used for monoprinting. Drop-cloth printing does add quite a bit of stiffness to the fabric because of the amount of paint used, but the effect is well worth it, and it's amazingly fun to do!

1. Using a separate spoon for each color, put a small amount of each paint color on the plate *(fig. 1)*.

2. With a palette knife, lightly push the paint around to create random patterns *(fig. 2)*. Tread lightly so you don't nick your plate. And don't blend too much or you'll lose the individual colors.

3. Pick up the plate and use it like a stamp, quickly touching it down on the fabric *(figs. 3 and 4)*.

4. Fold the fabric over on itself, and pat it to print the paint onto blank areas that weren't stamped *(figs. 5 and 6)*. You're basically creating monoprints from the areas you just stamped. Don't scrub the fabric together; that will cause you to lose patterning altogether.

5. Continue to add paint to the plate, one or two colors at a time, and stamp them onto the fabric in areas that need filling *(figs. 7 and 8)*. Take caution with how much you fold the fabric over. Just like putting the paint on the plate, the more you fold it over and print over top of previous areas, the more you blend the colors into a single tone. There is a limit to how much you can manipulate the fabric before it just turns into a strange mess.

6. "Clean" your palette knife by swiping it across any areas that could still use some paint.

7. When you're done adding paint, clean off your plate with water and a soft paper towel before the paint can dry.

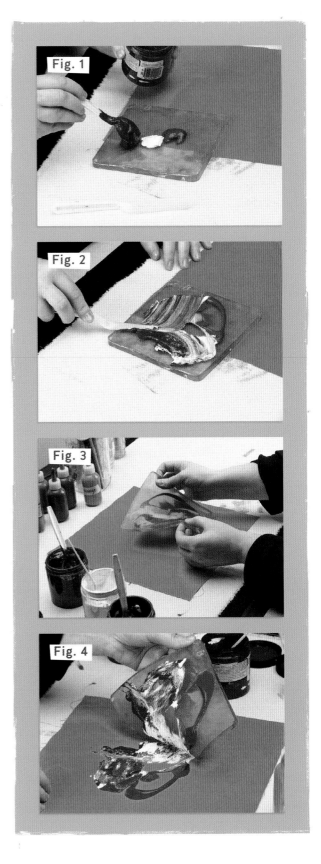

Fig. 1

Fig. 2

Fig. 3

Fig. 4

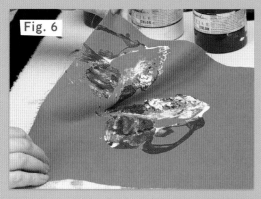

Fig. 5

Fig. 6

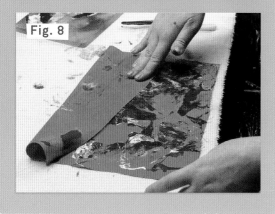

Fig. 7

Fig. 8

TIPS FOR DROP-CLOTH PRINTING

★ Choose no more than three colors for this technique. With more than that, you'll lose the distinct colors; they'll blend into one.

★ I like to use a Gelli Arts plate because it makes it really easy to move the paint around for random patterning. If you were to work directly on fabric for this technique, it would soak in before you had a chance to move it around. The plate gives you the freedom to arrange your paint.

★ This particular technique only works with a Gelli Arts Gel Printing Plate; you can't substitute a homemade gelatin plate. Homemade plates are very fragile and can't be picked up and moved around. Plus Gelli Arts plates are reusable, so you can monoprint whenever the mood strikes you.

★ On its own, this technique produces an admittedly very messy-looking result. This particular technique is well suited as the base layer in layered printing (see page 92).

THERMOFAX SCREEN PRINTING

I love screen printing. What I don't love is the time it takes to make a screen with emulsion and light exposure and a little prayer that I set up everything correctly. Thermofax screens completely take the intimidation out of screen printing, and I couldn't love them more.

YOU WILL NEED
- Thermofax screen
- Screen-printing paint
- Foam brush or hard-edged plastic scraper
- Fabric

These little beauties are silk screens with the images permanently burned into them. They are created with an old photocopy technology called a Thermofax machine. All that's needed is a Thermofax machine, a special screen called a Riso, and a black-and-white paper print of the image you want to use.

Over time, the machines have become scarce, making them expensive to purchase. Many artists who own machines will create screens—both ready-to-print images that they have designed or custom screens from your own artwork—for a fee (see Resources).

1. Place the screen shiny side down against the fabric.

2. Hold the screen down with one hand and squirt paint across it *(fig. 1)*.

3. Using a foam brush or hard-edged plastic scraper, push the paint through the screen *(figs. 2 and 3)*.

4. Lift one corner of the screen to see if you are satisfied with your print. If not, carefully lay the screen back down and swipe across the area that needs more defined printing a few more times.

5. Pull the screen off the fabric in one quick motion, being careful not to drag it across the fabric *(fig. 4)*.

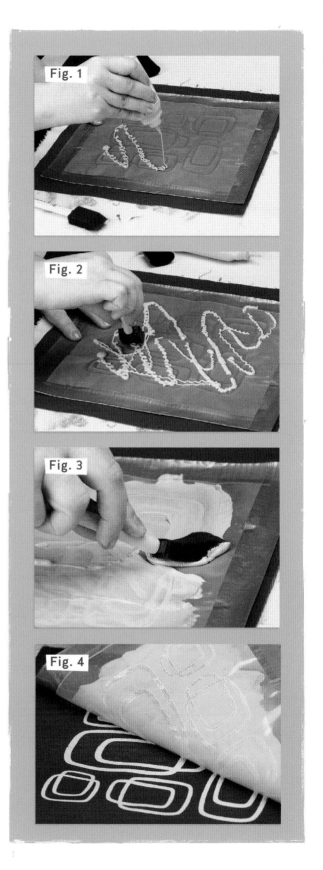

Fig. 1

Fig. 2

Fig. 3

Fig. 4

6. If you're done printing, wash the screen. If you're continuing to print, lay it down in the next area of the fabric and print again *(figs. 5 and 6)*.

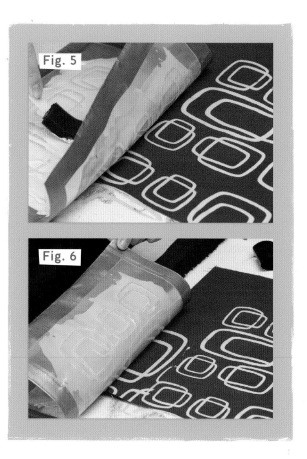

Fig. 5

Fig. 6

TIPS FOR THERMOFAX SCREEN PRINTING

★ Don't use a rubber squeegee as you would in traditional screen printing! Thermofax screens are made up of two layers, one is plastic and the other is mesh. A rubber squeegee creates too much friction and will quickly stress the bond between the layers, shortening the life of the screen.

★ Always use screen-printing paint or ink, never regular acrylic paint.

★ Use warm water and a sponge to wash the screens. Lay them flat to dry.

★ Allow the screen to dry completely after washing before printing with it again. Wet screens will produce blurry prints.

★ Store the screens flat to avoid causing permanent creases.

★ When you're printing an allover pattern, you have a couple of options. You can print in neat lines, or you can go random. If you go random, print off the edge of the fabric to give a more continuous look and intentionally space the prints unevenly.

★ When you're doing repeat printing, you don't need to wait for the paint to dry. Just be sure to check the back of the screen for wet paint marks before you lay it down on a new section of fabric.

SHADOW PRINTING

Shadows are great teachers for learning how to layer images. They can be solid or transparent, but you can always see what's beneath them. They are the inspiration behind what I call shadow printing. This technique produces an ombré effect. To create the effect, you print over portions of the fabric multiple times. It can be time-consuming, but the effect is beautiful and a great addition to layered printing (see page 92).

YOU WILL NEED
- Paint
- Squeeze bottle with tip
- Fabric

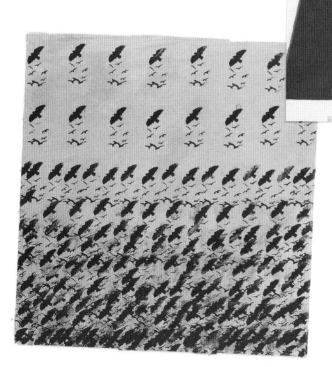

You can use any tool from the other techniques in this chapter with this technique. The instructions here are written using the drawing on fabric technique (page 42), but don't be afraid to wander off and use whatever strikes your fancy.

1. Identify the area of the fabric that you want to print. (You can split it into three equal portions by making a tick mark on your print surface canvas next to the fabric you're printing on.)

2. Write across the entire area *(fig. 1)*. Try to keep the writing in fairly straight lines.

3. Write across the bottom two-thirds of the fabric a second time *(fig. 2)*.

4. Write across just the bottom third of the fabric a third time *(fig. 3)*.

5. You may need to go back in and write a fourth or fifth time along the bottom third to create a more solid appearance to this section.

TIPS FOR SHADOW PRINTING

★ If you're stamping or Thermofax printing, choose an image with an open design that will let the base fabric show through. This creates more depth as the image is repeatedly stamped.

★ Old wood blocks work great for this technique.

★ This is recommended as a middle layer in layered printing (see page 92) because it's a strong printing method.

★ It's not necessary to let the prints dry in between stampings. You'll smudge the images a little, but this helps to create the shadowy effect.

★ Use more than one color of paint to create a variegated print.

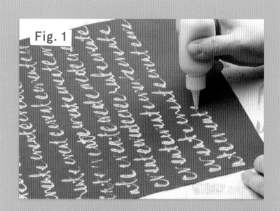

Fig. 1

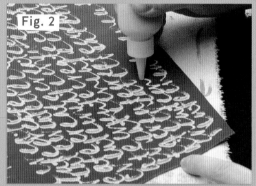

Fig. 2

Fig. 3

CARING FOR YOUR PRINTED FABRIC

Handprinted fabric is quite durable. Now, before you head out to lay it in direct sunlight and put it through the harshest cycle in your washing machine to see if I'm correct, let me explain.

When you print at home, you're using home-grade paint. By that I mean it's quite different from the paints that commercial printers use. Their paint is meant to survive a zombie apocalypse, and trust me when I say it's not something you want to handle in your home.

The paint you're using is certainly permanent. You can make it that way simply by ironing it with a really hot iron when it's dry. You can also wash it on a normal or gentle cycle, but know that it won't last as long as something you buy from the store if you wash it over and over.

I've found printed fabric to be very lightfast, but again, I'm not nailing it to the side of the house in direct light.

Be kind and sensible with your fabric, and it will last quite a long time.

What a Home Needs I. 20" × 20" (51 × 51 cm); machine piecing, handstitching, embellishing; commercial and handprinted fabrics, pillow form.

INTENTIONAL PRINTING IN ACTION

Kristin La Flamme

Kristin uses a combination of techniques in her work that crosses several territories: piecing, embroidery, and collage. Her work exudes a refined whimsy, one that is rooted in quiet movement. I created fabrics for her that mimic that kind of subtle movement in colors often seen in her work.

Printing technique: Thermofax screen printing (page 68)

"

I thoroughly enjoyed working with the fabric I received. The surface design was not so thick or stiff that it impeded my stitching and embroidery process. Not only do the two designs have a nice contrast in scale but both are unique and interesting.

My project is a pillow cover that combines a small painted and embroidered house, a vintage lace tablecloth, and a traditional star quilt block. I interpreted the swirly design in the tan fabric as stylized roots that surround the house, just as family roots and connections run deep. When I created it, I wasn't sure if I would finish the piece by mounting it on canvas, binding it like a mini quilt, or doing something else. The traditional aspects of the composition led me to make it into something practical—a pillow.

"

— *Kristin La Flamme*

CHAPTER 4

HANDSTITCHING

Embellishing your projects with handstitching is about far more than holding layers of fabric together. It's an opportunity to add additional design elements or colors. It's a finishing touch like no other. In this chapter I'll share some tips and tricks for handstitching and demonstrate my favorite stitches.

WHY HAND-STITCHING?

I'm a dedicated handstitcher. I believe I connect in a more solid way with my artwork when I'm forced to slow down and spend the time it takes to cover fabric in handstitching.

There is an intense meditative quality to the act, and no two stitches are the same, which leaves a more personal mark on the work. Plus it makes projects portable. In the little moments when I'm waiting for an appointment or visiting with friends, I can stitch on my project. It's a great way to squeeze in art making when you have a busy schedule.

This is not to say that I don't use machine stitching in my work. I do, but I almost always offset it with handstitching and keep it very simple.

I find that handstitching is becoming a lost art, and it's my sincere hope that you'll give it a shot. You may find that you like it as much as I do.

NEEDLES AND THREADS

Handstitching isn't something to be afraid of. If you've always wanted to try it but weren't sure where to begin, we're going to take away any angst you may have had by looking at the different types of threads available and what needles to use with them.

THREADS

There are many types of threads made for handstitching: cotton, linen, wool, silk, metallic. You can also get them in different weights and colors. The possibilities are endless. Let's make things a little more manageable by taking a look at some of the most common ones out there.

Embroidery Floss

Embroidery floss is made of up to six strands of thin thread. The strands are not tightly wound together, so you can choose the weight of your thread by pulling out as many strands as you'd like.

Some basic tools and materials for handstitching: embroidery floss, pearl cotton, sewing-machine thread, scissors, and needles.

Pearl Cotton

This is a two-ply thread that is twisted tightly together so that it can't be separated. It comes in different weights. The most common are size 5, size 8, and size 12. The larger the number, the thinner the thread.

Crochet Thread

Some of the smaller sizes of crochet and tatting thread are wonderful for handstitching. They come in a variety of colors, often variegated, and they are very smooth to stitch with since they are meant to slide easily for crocheting and tatting.

Sewing-Machine Thread

Yes, this can be used for handstitching as well! Its thin weight creates a more integrated look when used in a project, as it blends into the fabric more.

The sampler above shows how the threads differ:

RED THREAD = *size 5 pearl cotton*

LIGHT GRAY THREAD = *size 8 pearl cotton*

GREEN THREAD = *three strands of embroidery floss*

BROWN THREAD = *two strands of embroidery floss*

MULTICOLORED THREAD = *size 20 crochet thread*

WHITE THREAD = *sewing-machine thread*

NEEDLES

When stitching by hand, it's important to understand needles. You want to make sure to use a needle suited to the thread you are using. If the thread is too thick and the needle too small, the thread will become worn and may shred during stitching. If the thread is too thin and the needle too large, the needle will leave behind a visible hole that will detract from the stitching.

As with thread, needles are assigned numbers for sizes. The larger the number, the smaller the needle.

Chenille Needles

Chenille needles work well with thicker threads like pearl cotton. They have a larger eye than most other needles, but don't confuse them with tapestry needles. Tapestry needles have a blunt tip while chenilles have a sharp tip to pierce fabric.

Sharps

Sharps are shorter needles that work very well for detail stitching. This is the kind of needle I use when stitching with machine-weight thread.

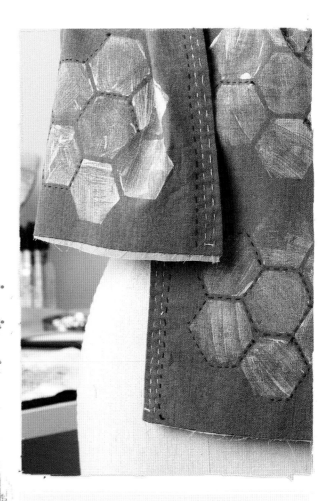

Visible handstitching along the edges creates a simple border. I partially stitched around the flower motifs as a reference to the broken stitches of the antique quilt that inspired my Granny's Garden Scarf (page 124).

TIPS FOR HANDSTITCHING

Here are a few things I've learned through experience that make handstitching a lot easier:

★ Don't use a length of thread much longer than 18" (45.5 cm). This will prevent tangling and fraying. Long lengths of thread get pulled through the layers of fabric more than shorter lengths, which can cause fraying and wear on the thread.

★ Don't lick the end of your thread to thread it through the needle! Over time you can rust the eye of the needle. Instead, pinch the thread flat very close to the end, and thread it through the needle. If you have trouble threading your needle, there are threaders available that can help.

★ Use embroidery scissors when cutting your thread. Large scissors make it hard to see where you are aiming, and it's very easy to cut a hole in your project.

★ Get a needle book to store your needles. This can be as simple as a couple of pieces of felt sewn together. Handstitching needles are easy to lose (and uncomfortable to find if you step on them), and a needle book will keep them handy.

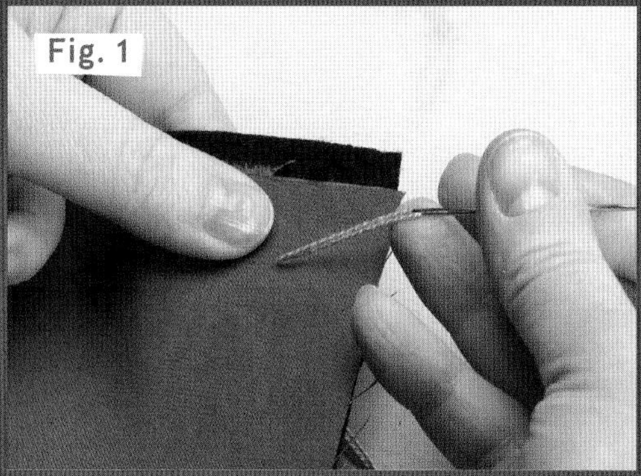

Fig. 1

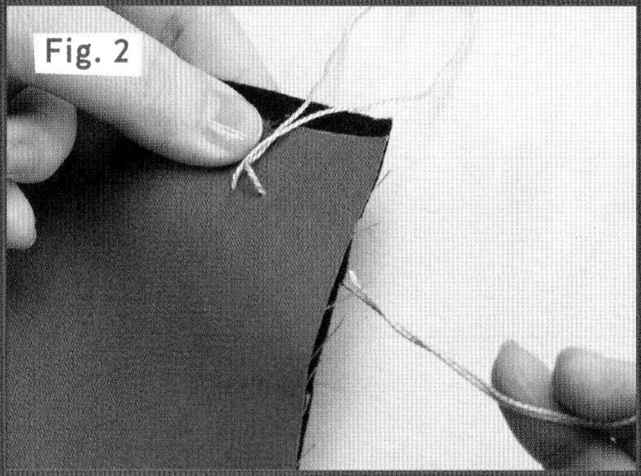

Fig. 2

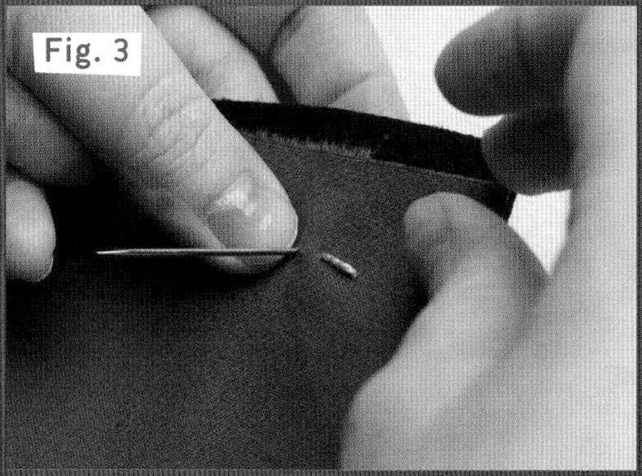

Fig. 3

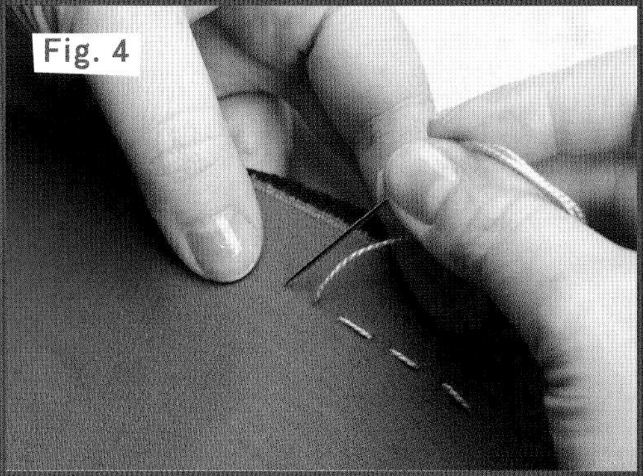

Fig. 4

TYPES OF STITCHES

Handstitching can be very elaborate and complicated or very simple and graphic. Both styles can have a great impact depending on the type of art you're making.

I prefer simple and graphic for my work. I treat stitching as another layer in the printing process, so I prefer it to blend into the work. Simple stitches combine well with the type of printing techniques I use.

The three main stitches I use are a straight stitch, a cross stitch, and a plus sign. All three are very simple and can be changed up simply by altering the thickness of the thread and the size of the stitches.

STRAIGHT STITCH

This simplest of stitches is quite versatile. Use it to outline shapes or stitch multiple rows to create texture.

1. Starting from the back, bring the needle to the front of the fabric and pull the thread through the layers of fabric *(fig. 1)*.

2. Go back down through the fabric a short distance from where you came up *(fig. 2)*. Be careful not to make the stitch too long or it will be loose and droop. About ¼" to ½" long is a good length.

3. Pull the thread through, then come back up to the front of the fabric *(fig. 3)*. Leave a gap between where the previous stitch ended and where the new one begins.

4. Repeat Steps 2 and 3 to create as many straight stitches as you'd like *(fig. 4)*.

CROSS STITCH

The cross, or X, stitch is one of the most popular embroidery stitches. Stitch them close together or space apart for different looks.

1. Starting from the back, bring the needle to the front of the fabric and pull the thread through the layers of fabric *(fig. 5)*.

2. Go back down through the fabric at a diagonal from where you came up to the front of the fabric *(figs. 6 and 7)*.

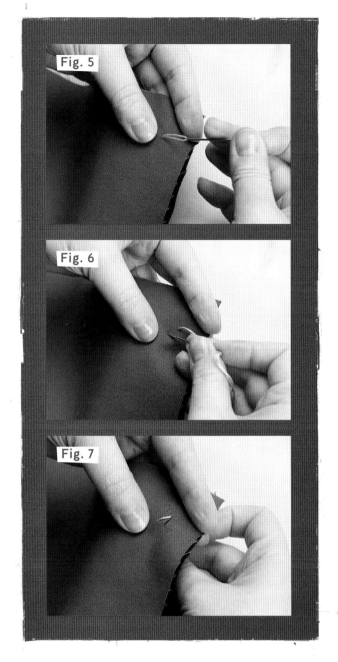

Fig. 5

Fig. 6

Fig. 7

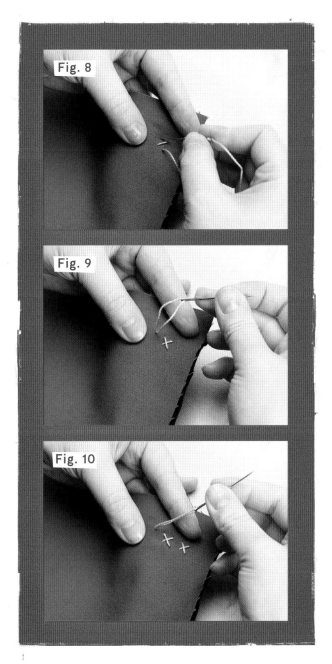

Fig. 8

Fig. 9

Fig. 10

3. Come back up to the front of the fabric to the right of where you last pulled the thread to the back. Go back down through the fabric at a diagonal from where you came up. Line this up with the top "edge" of the existing stitch *(fig. 8)*.

4. Bring the needle to the front of the fabric a small distance from the previous X stitch. Start again at the top "edge" of the X *(fig. 9)*.

5. Follow Steps 2 through 4 to create multiple cross stitches *(fig. 10)*.

PLUS-SIGN STITCH

The plus sign is similar to the cross stitch and can be used interchangeably.

1. Starting from the back, bring the needle to the front of the fabric and pull the thread through the layers of fabric *(fig. 11)*.

2. Go back down through the fabric to complete a vertical straight stitch. Come back up to the front of the fabric a small distance to the right from the vertical stitch, lined up roughly with the middle of it *(fig. 12)*.

3. Cross over the vertical stitch and go back down through the fabric to complete a horizontal straight stitch.

4. Repeat Steps 1 through 3 to complete as many plus signs and you would like *(fig. 13)*.

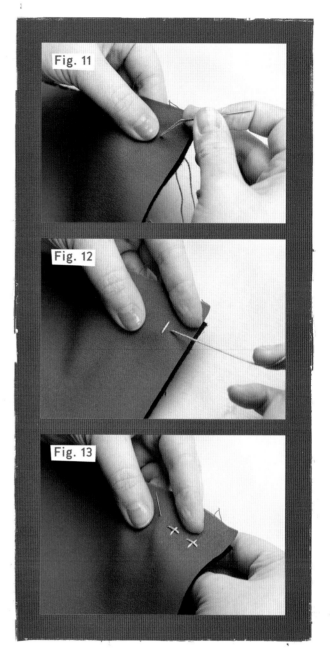

The sample here shows all three stitches. It was stitched with Aurifil's Lana thread, which is a 50/50 wool acrylic. It's one of my favorite threads because it gives a slightly fuzzy look to the stitches but is very strong because of the acrylic.

MACHINE STITCHING

You may be wondering what in the world this is doing here. I've proclaimed myself to be a disciple of handstitching and have tried to convert you to my ways. The truth is I once fancied myself a budding free-motion quilter. Through a series of arguments with my machine and the final admission that handstitching better defines the vision I hold for my work, I found myself nudging my machine out of the picture.

But my attitude toward the tools in my studio is that if something is taking up space, it's going to get used and earn its keep. If it doesn't, then it's shown the door. I was determined to find a place for some sort of machine stitching in my work because I'd spent a decent chunk of change on the machine and, honestly, the speed it offers is very appealing.

In the end, I came to a truce in which very basic straight stitching on a machine finds its way into some pieces. Most of the time it's buried in the background, but I admit that I really enjoy the texture it provides. It will never replace handstitching for me, but I'm pleased that we've come to an understanding.

Some projects, like the Beanbag Desk Weights (page 108) are better served by machine stitching for the construction portion. The seams need to be really solid so the pellets don't work their way out. When strength is an issue, I always machine stitch to make sure everything stays where it belongs.

TIPS FOR MACHINE STITCHING

I'm in no way an expert at machine stitching and to pretend otherwise would make me a liar. But I can offer you tips on how I like to use stitching in my work.

If you're like me and you find the machine to be an uneasy friend, give these a shot and see if they work for you. (Note that these tips don't apply to construction stitching, meaning stitching that is used to assemble a project, as in the Beanbag Desk Weights)

★ Machine stitching can be used as a layer when printing complex pieces. It creates wonderful texture to build off of. (I discuss this in the layered printing chapter, page 92.)

★ Use longer stitch lengths (between 3.0 and 4.0) to mimic handstitching.

★ Use a different color thread in the top spool than in the bobbin. You'll get dots of the bobbin thread peeking through, creating a tiny pop of color.

★ I don't bury my ends; I let them hang loose. I love the texture and organic feeling this adds.

★ If you're stitching several rows on a piece (like for the Coffee Talk Hoops, page 112), use the foot on your machine to guesstimate the width of rows. Don't get bogged down with worrying about them being exact; let the fabric move and let the rows shift slightly.

★ Use a walking foot if you have one. I normally stitch the fabric alone, meaning I don't use backing or stabilizer. A walking foot helps keep things moving under the needle.

★ If you plan to stitch rows over an entire piece of fabric, start at an edge to establish a straight-ish line. Switch sides every other row to help control puckering. Pausing periodically to press the fabric with steam will help keep things flat. (But really, a little pucker is not the end of the world. It's fabric, after all, and that is just its nature.)

★ Use good quality thread. I use Aurifil the majority of the time because the colors are rich and the thread is smooth.

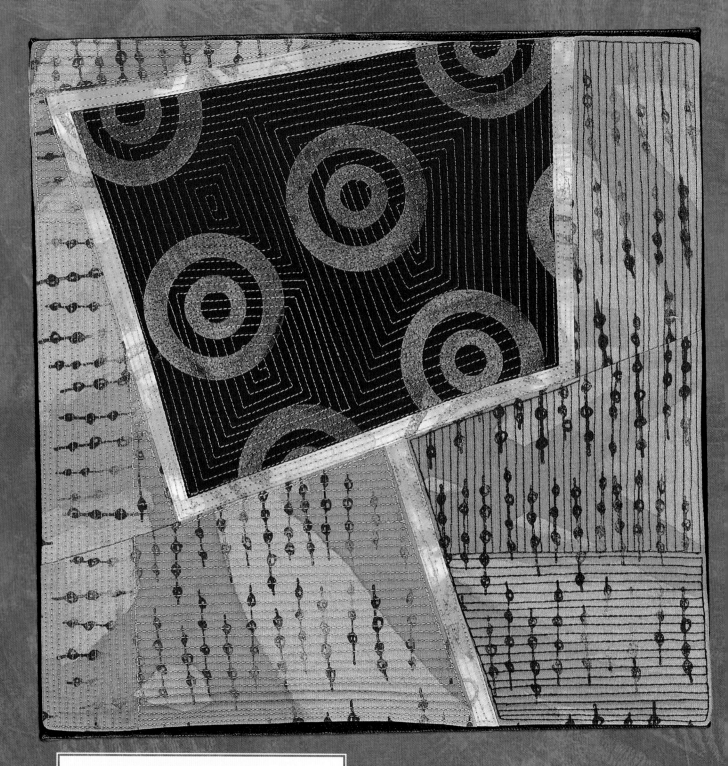

Portals #4. 12" × 12" (30.5 × 30.5 cm); machine piecing, machine stitching; handprinted fabric, canvas.

INTENTIONAL PRINTING IN ACTION

Lisa Call

The precision with which Lisa approaches her work is stunning. Her piecing is impeccable, and she embraces abstraction in the most beautiful of ways. While she is well known for using her hand-dyed solid fabric in her work, I felt confident I could print fabric for her that would still play well with her trademark style.

66

I enjoy that fabric is much more flexible and versatile than many other mediums. I use exclusively 100% cotton woven fabric and love the inherent grid in the woven structure of the material, which I incorporate into my compositions.

As I have grown as an artist, I have explored other mediums, but they don't provide the same tactile experience that fabric does. One doesn't often run their hand across an oil painting, yet I am constantly stroking the fabric as I work. I miss this part of the process when painting or drawing.

Working with painted textiles allows me the freedom to explore the beauty of the hand-drawn line while maintaining my connection to the woven fabric that is an integral part of my art-making experience.

99

— *Lisa Call*

Printing techniques: *Top: Thermofax screen printing (page 68); bottom: Thermofax screen printing and fluid printing (page 46).*

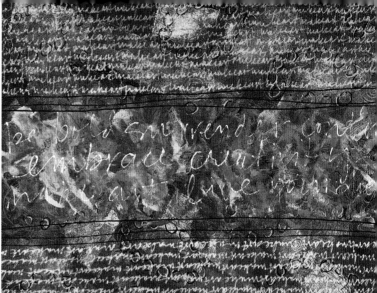

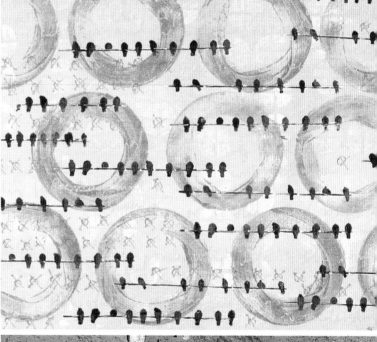

CHAPTER 5

LAYERED PRINTING

Now that we've learned several different ways to print on fabric, it's time to dive into the magical bit of printing: layered printing! While I have great affection for each technique on its own, I fully admit that they can sometimes feel one-note. Some techniques are just begging for something more, which is where layered printing comes in.

TWO TYPES OF LAYERED PRINTING

Layered printing simply means printing more than one image and more than one color on a single piece of fabric. The fabric is printed in stages, which are referred to as layers. How much you print depends on your end goal. I use two different styles of layered printing: quiet layered printing and intense layered printing

Quiet layered printing (QLP) refers to a more restrained style of layered printing. It follows a regimen every single time and is the way I most often print for projects. In fact, every project in this book uses this type of layered printing. I call it "quiet" because it hits the sweet spot of creating printed pieces that can be cut up and stitched while still retaining the printed imagery as a whole.

Intense layered printing (ILP) is quite the opposite. There is no set definition of when to stop or how much to add. And when you're done, it's the end product—the final piece of art. Quite often

I incorporate machine and handstitching into the piece to add texture and make it feel more complete. My preferred method of presentation is to fuse it to a pre-stretched canvas and then paint the edges of the canvas. ILP begins exactly the same way that QLP does, but beyond that, it's a free-for-all.

Because I wanted to show you how controlled printing can really serve you in creating work, I used QLP in all the projects. (We came close to ILP in the Meditation Cloth project, page 134, but we kept the printing simple, so it's not quite there. That project is a good start to move to ILP if you like the idea of it.) But to completely skip over ILP would do you a disservice because that is your place to really push the limits of the work and experiment. We're going to walk through both, and to illustrate clearly the difference between the two, I'm going to use the same fabric and beginning printing on both. Seeing how a piece changes based on unique choices is the best way to understand each one.

Ready?

> **TIP:** *The samples printed in this section are 18"
> (45.5 cm) squares. I chose this size because it's the size
> needed for the canvas that the final ILP piece is
> attached to. The principles will work on any size
> fabric you wish to use.*

This Fabric-Tile Triptych (page 128), which features stamping, Thermofax screen printing, and decay printing, is an example of quiet layered printing.

QUIET LAYERED PRINTING

When you're working on projects, especially smaller ones like many of those in this book, you want to think about where you place your printing so you can maximize the impact of it. If you plan the printing, you'll get the effect you're after.

For this example, I'm printing fabric that will be cut to make oversized drink coasters (6" [15 cm] squares). It's a simple project that is a perfect showcase for your printed fabric. I want the printed fabric to appear organic, meaning I don't want to fuss with making sure the images are lined up exactly in the middle of each coaster. I want each one to capture a portion of the image and for each to be different but still connected to the others. Printing a single piece of fabric will accomplish this.

Because this fabric will be cut into smaller pieces, we need to restrain the printing. When fabric is reduced to smaller pieces, it automatically becomes more energetic than when it was larger. This is because you have a much more focused view of it. If we keep the printing on the quiet side, we can add stitching or embellishments after it is cut up without crossing into the land of tacky.

I always follow the same set of printing guidelines for this style of layered printing. It's by no means the *only* way to go about this, but it has served me well, and it has taken the fear out of how to begin working on a blank piece of fabric. QLP consists of three layers, and each one contains a color and image element that help build an interesting piece of fabric.

BASE LAYER: *White paint and Thermofax screen printing. The incomplete printing of the image makes this layer feel airy.*

BASE LAYER (LAYER 1)

This is the first layer you print on your fabric.

Base-Layer Color Considerations

In order to create depth in your printed fabric, it's necessary to print both a dark color and a contrasting color at some stage. I like to do these on either the base or middle layer because they can be broken up by additional printing and not take over the composition.

Base-Layer Image Considerations

Small-scale, open images work best on the base layer. Making the prints imperfect is a good idea as well since it breaks up the image. The goal is to allow the color of the base fabric to show through; you don't want to completely cover the fabric in a solid wall of paint, or it will begin to feel like a piece of armor. Print across the entire piece of fabric, all the way off the edges.

MIDDLE LAYER (LAYER 2)

This is the second layer you print on your fabric, over top of the base layer.

Middle-Layer Color Considerations

Again, it's best to use either a darker or contrast color on this layer. Be cautious if you're printing the darker color here because, if you go too dark, it will act as a shock and will be the main thing you see when you look at the fabric. A darker color does not necessarily mean black. It can simply be a darker shade of the base fabric or base layer. For example, if your base fabric is medium blue, use a dark blue for your dark color. If your base layer is pink, use a dark pink for your dark color.

Middle-Layer Image Considerations

Large-scale, semi-open imagery as well as swipes of paint made by brayers or foam brushes work well here. Large-scale images help break up the overall look of the fabric and create movement. You still want to allow the layers beneath it to show, so choose something that is open but has more bold-ness to it. Print across the entire piece of fabric, all the way off the edges.

TOP LAYER (LAYER 3)

This is the last layer you print on your fabric. It's printed over top of the base and middle layers.

Top-Layer Color Considerations

This layer should play off the color of the base fabric. By this I mean it should be one of the colors close to it or opposite it on the color wheel. Which one you choose depends on if you want a serene composition (a color close to it on the color wheel) or an energetic composition (a color opposite it). Because we've worked carefully on the other two layers, we can introduce a huge pop of color at this stage if we wish.

MIDDLE LAYER: *Brown paint and color-wash printing. The darker color and the color-wash technique provide a bold image without blocking out too much of the base layer. And we get an added bonus of color interplay between the three colors now present. Where the brown appears on the rust-orange fabric, it's quite dark. But where it streaks across the white paint, it's a pale brown.*

TOP LAYER: *Bright blue paint and decay printing with papier mâché lids.*

Top-Layer Image Considerations

Medium-scale, very graphic images work well for this final layer. This is the layer in which you add your focal point, so you can block out as much of the layers underneath as you want. I like to leave some openness to them so all the colors and shapes can play off each other. This layer rules the roost and directs the viewer where to look, but the goal is to add it as a focal point, not as a way to cover up all that is underneath. Since I know I want to cut up the fabric to use as coasters, I've printed them in a fairly orderly way, but I've not stressed about making sure that they are in perfect rows and columns. I'll get a blue circle in each coaster but they won't all be in the exact same spot.

INTENSE LAYERED PRINTING

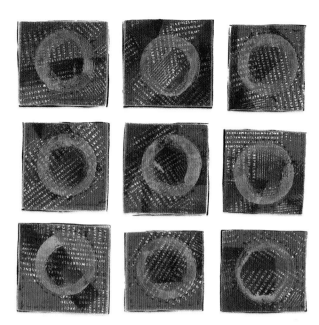

Now let's take a look at what happens if we don't stop at the top layer in the QLP example.

I know what you're thinking now; you're wondering how to know when to stop. It can be difficult to gauge when you first start working this way; but trust me, after you've taken one too far, you'll learn to pay better attention. I'm going to do my best to help you avoid getting to that point.

The best advice I can give you about ILP is this: add one more bold print and then make the rest about adding details. By adding one more bold print, you're creating an anchor to build your extra details around. Not everything you add will be standing up and shouting for attention, but you'll be filling in the gaps, and this adds a very complex look to the fabric. Remember, with ILP we're creating the final product to be displayed, so details are essential.

To make the coasters, I cut the fabric into 6" (15 cm) squares, laid them over two layers of felt, and stitched them together. It's a very cohesive set of coasters, and we have accomplished our goal of interesting color combinations and an even distribution of imagery across all of them.

TROUBLESHOOTING LAYERED PRINTING

Before we move on to the intense layered printing, I want to show you two examples of printing that have some troubles and explain what went wrong.

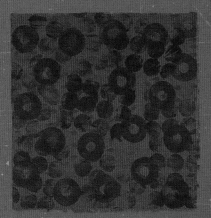

The second example does a little better in the color department, but it has issues with scale and type of image. Not only are they all circles, but they're all the same size. It doesn't tell a story like our QLP piece does; it's just flailing about without focus. Without any variation in type of image or scale, you simply can't create an interesting narrative with the fabric.

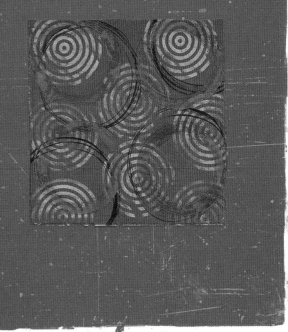

The first example struggles with its color scheme. The base layer was printed in a light orange that just can't hold its own against the rust-orange fabric. The paint lacks opacity, so it nearly disappears. The middle layer and top layer are better in terms of contrast, but they are too close to each other to create any interest. The lack of change in color makes the piece quite boring and one-note.

LAYER 4

After adding some subtle machine stitching to the top layer from the QLP example, I drew outlines in lime green paint around the blue circles. I wanted to bring more attention to the blue circles, and a light outline helps give them more presence. I used lime green because, even though it might not be easy to see from far away, the machine thread I stitched with before printing is a light green, and the lime green outline helps pull that forward.

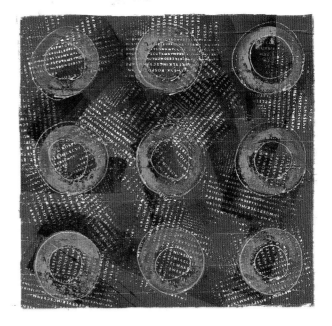

LAYER 5

With an olive green paint, I painted fifteen X shapes in three rows centered on the fabric simply by dipping a foam brush into paint and freehand painting them. Once you have this many layers, you're basically doing a dance of pushing the color and composition back and pulling it forward. Printing our anchor image in a dark color oppresses what is already there. For this piece, the X's in the darker green act as our anchor image. Remember that we want to create depth, and the way to do that is with dark colors. Also, by doing this, we create the opportunity to lighten it back up with more details.

LAYER 6

I outlined the X shapes by drawing around them with black paint. I was a little tentative at this stage. I wanted to bring out the X's, and because I used a very low-opacity paint in Layer 4, I needed to give them definition. The outlining accomplished that, but it was still too dark. Time to lighten things up.

LAYER 7

I decided a little doodling was in order for this layer, so I doodled on the light blue circles with darker blue paint to make them recede a little bit. But I began to feel that there was too much darkness around the X's, that they didn't stand out enough. In order to combat this, I added a second outline inside the first with white paint.

I added the doodling in to create some movement and playfulness. At this stage, I really wasn't sure if I should add more, so I took the most important step in this process: I tacked it up on my design board and walked away from it.

I can't stress how helpful some distance from your work is. The break allows you to gain some clarity so you can make stronger decisions about how (or if) you should continue on with the printing.

LAYER 8

After some alone time, the fabric told me what it needed. Even though I had created the X shapes as an anchor image, they were still competing with the rust fabric. They needed a frame to block out the background. So I took red paint (which typically has pretty low opacity) and shadow printed two strips along the top and bottom to create a frame. Then I drew over them with black paint in a grid to give them more presence.

What I ended up with is incredibly layered. I think presentation is just as important as the art itself, so I fused the fabric to a 2" (5 cm) deep pre-stretched canvas. I painted the edges black, allowing the paint to trail up on the edges of the fabric, and drew white circles on the sides of the canvas. To keep attention on the X's, I titled it 15x (times).

I admit this is a bold piece, but I love it. It has a heartbeat all its own, and it keeps my attention.

If it doesn't ring your bell, it could be because it has *a lot* going on. Intense layered printing works

equally well with fewer layers and calmer colors. Here are a few more examples of printed fabric that went beyond the three basic layers of QLP.

These examples show just how versatile layered printing can be. You can make it do your bidding no matter how crazy or restrained you want to be. The only limitation is your willingness to experiment. So let yourself go and see where it takes you!

My Town's Courthouse. 23½" × 17½" (59.5 × 44.5 cm);
fused appliqué, machine stitching, handstitching;
commercial and handprinted fabrics.

INTENTIONAL PRINTING IN ACTION

Pamela Allen

Many years ago I took a class with Pamela Allen, and I recall being horrified by the way she threw pattern and color together with abandon. At the time, I couldn't wrap my mind around it, but I'll never forget the look she gave me that said, "You'll get it one day." And I do; I get it now. Pamela's love of pattern and color is legendary. The fabric I printed for her was created with this in mind.

"

When I received the fabric, I could see right away that Lynn had me in mind. The colors, deep turquoise and purple, are my colors. Serendipity assisted, as well, in that I had been concentrating on cityscapes for the last several months, and the prints were perfect for such a scene.

I chose to create a piece based on the courthouse in my hometown. The fabric was ideal for decorative details on the dome roof and windows, as well as the surrounding nineteenth-century houses.

I used darker fabrics in some areas to accentuate the richness of the color palette and very light fabrics in other areas for high contrast. Finally, some well-placed 'bubble' quilting repeats the circles in Lynn's print and helps unify the whole piece.

— *Pamela Allen*

"

Printing techniques: Top: Thermofax screen printing (page 68) and drawing on fabric (page 42); bottom: drawing on fabric.

Now that we know plenty of techniques and have given ourselves a lot of room to think about what we like and what we don't, we're going to translate all of that knowledge into some projects. The ones in this book range from wearables to useful objects to "just because." There's sure to be a few that will strike your fancy and get your creativity revved up!

PRINTING FOR A PROJECT

Are you ready to start making stuff? I am! But before we start flinging paint and fabric, I want to pause and give us some focus. The whole endeavor we have set out on is to print fabric that we can use successfully in projects. That means we don't end up setting it on fire because we can't stand the way it turned out.

I do want to talk a little bit about how I approach creating projects because I might have some quirks that are different from how you work.

EDGES AND SEAMS

The majority of my work has raw edges. I love the frayed look of fabric; it feels natural to me to let it do its thing. That means I often work to the finished size rather than adding seam allowances to the fabric dimensions. Some of the projects in this book don't need seam allowances, while others require them. I will always note the fabric size needed and if it includes any extra for seams or finishing, so you can choose to add more if you'd like to finish your project differently than I did.

WHEN AND WHAT TO PRINT

I only print fabric when I'm making a project. What? Let me say that again: I only print fabric when I'm making a project. I save every bit of leftovers for collages and other projects (we'll be making one of these as well), but to keep my resources, time, and stash in line, I work with purpose.

I often print a project after I've assembled it. I find this creates unified work in some instances because the printing crosses over seams. If this makes you wildly uncomfortable, print the fabric before you assemble the project, but keep in mind that the finished project might look different from the photo in the book (which is not a bad thing!).

EVERYTHING IN ITS PLACE

I'm a fuser. I layer Mistyfuse fusible web on many of my projects to keep things in place. It's the only fusible web I use because it's so easy to handstitch through. Fusing also means that I don't need to pin my work to hold it together, so I'm not constantly stabbing myself with extra pins while I stitch. It's part self-preservation and part convenience. Mistyfuse does not have a paper backing like other fusibles, so it takes some getting used to, but it's worth the effort. See Working with Mistyfuse (below) for more on using this helpful material.

WORKING WITH MISTYFUSE

Mistyfuse is a fusible web. Fusible web acts like a glue to hold layers of fabric together. It's placed between two layers of fabric (or between fabric and felt/batting) and then ironed to make it melt. When it melts, it fuses the two layers together, creating a permanent bond. It essentially takes the place of basting or pinning layers together.

Mistyfuse is unique in that it is very, very lightweight. Because it's lightweight, the bond doesn't interfere with handstitching, meaning it's really easy for me to push a needle through all the layers without feeling like I'm trying to sew through a brick. If you're not concerned about handstitching, you can use a heavier-weight fusible web.

Never let your iron directly touch fusible web! It will create a mess. If you don't have a layer of fabric on top of the Mistyfuse, place a piece of parchment paper over it. The fusible will not stick to it, and your iron will be protected.

SIZE MATTERS

The scale of the print you use for a project depends entirely on the project itself. If the work is larger, you can easily incorporate any scale into it, but if you're working smaller, you really need to be conscious of the image size you work with. Images that are on the medium to large scale will be lost, so you'll want smaller-scale prints. The goal is to feature your print, not lose it when you assemble the project. (See the printing and design considerations for each project for more information.)

ROOM TO EXPLORE

In the materials section for each project, I list the colors of fabric and paint that I used. These are for your reference in case you see a combination you'd like to duplicate, but they are by no means written in stone. I encourage you to explore and pick the colors that speak the loudest to you.

FOR YOUR CONSIDERATION

At the start of each project, I'll quickly talk about the printing and design considerations needed for that particular project. All of the printing was thought out so that it would complement the project. Don't be intimidated! It's an easy habit to get into, and once you do, you'll find that you're making more work that you're pleased with.

Now that you have a better understanding of how I work, you can adjust the project instructions that don't suit your taste.

Let's start making stuff!

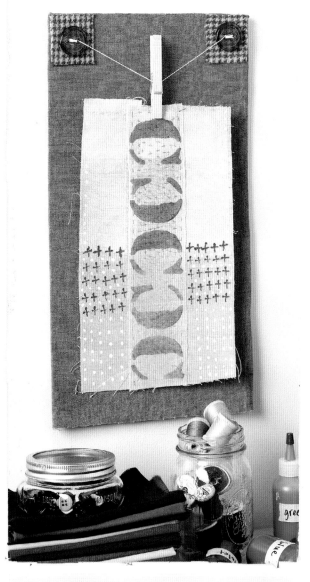

Creating a Meditation Cloth (page 134) is a great way to explore the ideas of intentional printing.

BEANBAG DESK WEIGHTS

FINISHED MEASUREMENTS

- One desk weight measures about 5½" × 5½" (14 × 14 cm).

PRINTING TECHNIQUES

- Stamping (page 52)
- Drawing on Fabric (page 42)

YOU WILL NEED (FOR ONE DESK WEIGHT)

- ¼ yd (23 cm) olive-colored fabric
- Yellow ochre, white, black, and blue textile paint
- Self-adhesive foam
- Chevron template (page 148)
- 9½" (24 cm) long × 2½" (6.5 cm) wide piece of cardboard
- Foam brushes
- Squeeze bottles with tips
- Poly-Pellets (You can also use rice or dried beans, but I find the plastic pellets last much longer.)
- Small funnel
- Sewing machine
- Size 8 pearl cotton embroidery thread and needle
- Scissors

There is something inherently charming about beanbags that we never quite outgrow, isn't there? Not only are they a source of entertainment, but they also serve a purpose. I'm something of a beanbag hoarder, only I call them desk weights. (Sounds more adult, doesn't it?)

My desk weights perch on top of piles on my desk, helping me keep things in place. If you're a sewist, you can also use these to hold down your patterns while you cut. I bet you can find lots of other uses for these wobbly little weights.

[DESIGN & PRINTING CONSIDERATIONS]

For a project this small, an allover graphic pattern works really well because you don't have to be fussy about where it lands.

We're printing both sides of the desk weight as a single piece of fabric rather than printing two single squares. This allows us to establish a continuous pattern that, when split up into two halves, will appear seamless.

We're also keeping the scale of the design on the smaller side. This helps our little project appear full of detail.

1. Cut or tear a 13" (33 cm) long × 6½" (16.5 cm) wide piece of olive green fabric. (Measurements include seam allowances.)

2. Create your chevron stamp from self-adhesive foam and cardboard. Freehand draw it or use the provided template (fig. 1). (Remember to trace it on your foam backward, so it will print in the same way as in the sample.)

3. Apply yellow ochre paint to your chevron stamp and, beginning at the bottom of the piece of fabric, stamp a repeat across the length of the fabric. Stamp the prints fairly close together, but don't stress about having consistent spacing (fig. 2). Let dry.

4. Put some white paint in a squeeze bottle and outline the stamped chevron pattern with a line of white (fig. 3). Let dry.

5. Put some black paint in a squeeze bottle and draw a small random circle pattern between the white outlines. Let dry.

6. Put some blue paint in a squeeze bottle and fill in the black circles (fig. 4). Let dry.

7. Cut the fabric in half to create two 6½" (16.5 cm) × 6½" (16.5 cm) squares, and pin with printed sides together.

8. With your sewing machine, sew around the edges with about a ½" (1.3 mm) seam allowance, leaving a 1½" (3.8 cm) opening along one of the sides.

9. Turn the desk weight right side out, gently using scissors to push the corners into points.

10. Using a small funnel, fill the desk weight about three-quarters full with plastic pellets.

11. Pin the opening shut with a straight pin.

12. Using size 8 pearl cotton, handstitch a line around the edge of the desk weight to create a "frame" and close the opening.

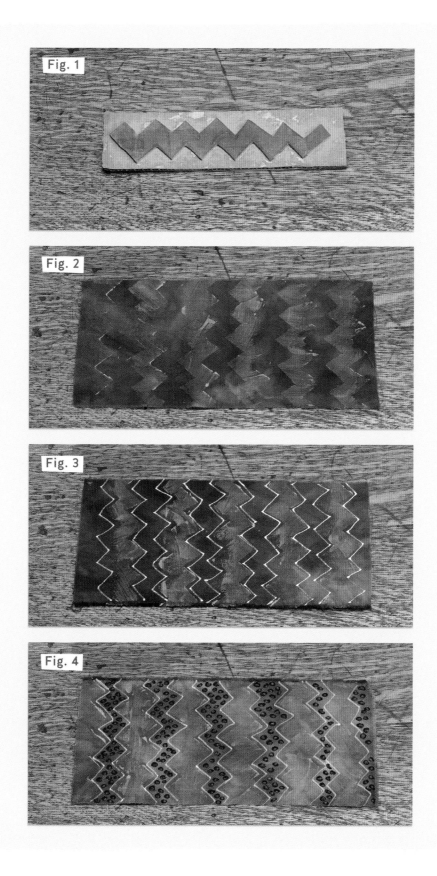

Fig. 1

Fig. 2

Fig. 3

Fig. 4

COFFEE TALK HOOPS

FINISHED MEASUREMENTS

- Hoop shown on page 114 measures 6" (15 cm) in diameter.

PRINTING TECHNIQUES

- Drawing on Fabric (page 42)
- Splatter Painting (page 48)
- Thermofax Screen Printing (page 68)

YOU WILL NEED (FOR ONE HOOP)

- 6" (15 cm) embroidery hoop
- ½ yd (45.5 cm) khaki fabric
- Turquoise Dye-Na-Flow paint
- White and brown textile paint
- Sewing machine
- Sewing-machine thread in a color close to the fabric
- "Coffee Cup" Thermofax screen (page 149)
- Foam brushes
- Paint pipette
- Squeeze bottle with tip
- Fabric-marking chalk or marking pen
- Craft glue

Embroidery hoops offer the perfect presentation method for small artwork. They are especially attractive in a grouping. I have an affection for old metal hoops, but wooden ones work just as well.

I combined my undying loves for coffee and writing in this project. The goal of the writing is not to give the viewer epic prose but rather to add movement to the piece, so write whatever you like. Once you're done with the project, the writing will fade nicely into the background.

DESIGN & PRINTING CONSIDERATIONS

When you're creating a grouping like this, offsetting the focal image–in this case, the coffee cup–in each hoop so it's sometimes only partially shown keeps the repeating image from getting stale.

This kind of project is a good candidate for splatter printing. Because of the small window the hoop provides, it breaks up the splatter pattern and makes it easier on the eyes.

Splatter painting mimics coffee spills and stains, continuing the theme set by the coffee cup images. Don't feel that you have to be literal with the color when you use this kind of connection. Blue and green coffee doesn't exist, but it creates a nice punch of color on the piece while maintaining the integrity of the design.

TIP: *If you use a different-size hoop, you will need to adjust the size of the fabric. Take the size of the hoop and add 2½" (6.5 cm) to each side to determine the size fabric you need. So for a 6" (15 cm) hoop, we need an 11" (28 cm) square of fabric.*

1. Cut or tear khaki fabric into an 11" (28 cm) square.

2. Using a thread close in tone to the fabric, machine stitch lines onto the 11" (28 cm) square of fabric approximately ½" (1.3 cm) apart *(fig. 1)*.

3. Using white paint and the squeeze bottle, write between the lines you just stitched. Work across the entire piece of fabric even though the edges will be trimmed down at the end *(fig. 2)*. Write in every other space so it doesn't appear too crowded. Let dry.

4. Using a paint pipette, splatter paint turquoise fluid paint randomly across the fabric *(fig. 3)*. Let dry.

5. With marking chalk, trace the inside of the outer piece of the embroidery hoop onto the fabric. There are two parts to the hoop, and you want to mark the area that will show once it's assembled.

6. Print the "Coffee Cup" Thermofax screen in the center of the marked circle with brown paint *(fig. 4)*. Let the fabric dry, then iron.

7. Assemble dry and ironed fabric into the embroidery hoop, tugging the fabric around the edges so it is taut.

8. Trim the edges to about ¾" (2 cm). Clip them every ½" (1.3 cm) or so to make the fabric easier to turn over the edges of the hoop.

9. Apply craft glue along the center of the overhanging fabric, and quickly fold over the edges of the hoop. Press firmly against the hoop so the fabric adheres.

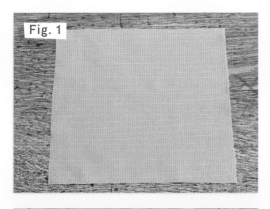

Fig. 1

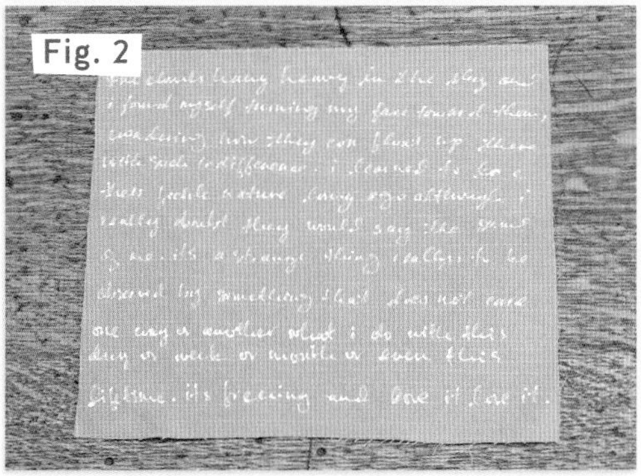

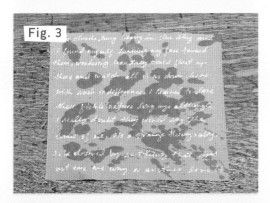

Fig. 2

Fig. 3

Fig. 4

TIPS: *The last step is a bit fussy. But it's necessary to secure the fabric inside the hoop and keep it from shifting over time. Apply a medium amount of glue so the fabric will grab to the hoop. Be patient, especially if you are using a metal hoop.*

The great thing about embroidery hoops is that they are ready to hang on the wall just the way they are and don't require any additional hardware. If you like, you can tie a ribbon around the top of the hoop screw to hang it.

THERMOFAX ALTERNATIVE

Because the coffee-cup motif used in this project is a fairly simple design, you could create a stamp instead of using a Thermofax screen. I've provided a template of the coffee-cup motif on page 149 if you'd like to try this. See page 52 for more on creating stamps with self-adhesive foam.

COLOR-BLOCK TABLE RUNNER

FINISHED MEASUREMENTS

- 12" (30.5 cm) wide × 40" (101.5 cm) long.

PRINTING TECHNIQUES

- Drawing on Fabric (page 42)
- Thermofax Screen Printing (page 68)
- Decay Printing (page 56)

YOU WILL NEED

- ¼ yd (23 cm) each of blue and brown fabric
- Light blue, metallic blue, and white textile paint
- Squeeze bottle with tip
- Felt
- Mistyfuse
- Iron
- "Birds on a Wire" Thermofax screen (see Resources)
- Foam brushes
- 7½" (19 cm) and 6" (15 cm) diameter papier mâché lids
- Machine-weight sewing thread and hand-embroidery needles
- White seed beads (optional)
- Rectangular brown beads (optional)
- Thin hand-sewing needle and beading thread (optional)

Table runners serve double duty by protecting your furniture and adding a distinct design element to the room's décor. We're giving the table runner an updated spin by handprinting the imagery. This project is a good example of using colors that are low-key and quiet. Each color complements the others, and when combined into a single project, they produce a piece that is rich in detail and depth.

[DESIGN & PRINTING CONSIDERATIONS]

This project demonstrates working in a fairly quiet color palette. All of the colors relate to each other, and we've added punches of color through the use of white paint and orange and black threads. For larger projects like this that you want to settle nicely into your décor, this type of color scheme creates the kind of quiet assimilation you're looking for.

We mimicked the long lines of the piece with the "Birds on a Wire" Thermofax screen, but it's important to break up all the linear elements to keep the work interesting. Printing the circles over the seams accomplishes this for us.

The white paint used to print the circles is not very opaque. This keeps it from turning into a shocking element, instead allowing it to add contrast without overwhelming the other colors, since the base is allowed to show through.

1. Cut or tear two pieces of fabric from each color, each measuring 6" (15 cm) × 20" (51 cm). (Measurements don't include seam allowances; add them in if you want to bind your work.)

2. On the two pieces of blue fabric, write text with the light blue paint. Let dry.

3. Cut your felt base to the finished size of 12" (30.5 cm) × 40" (101.5 cm). (Consider using a different color felt to add contrast to the fabric you chose.)

4. Lay Mistyfuse over top of the felt.

5. Arrange the fabric in a checkerboard pattern. Lay the brown unprinted pieces down first and the text-printed pieces over them *(fig. 1)*.

6. Fuse fabric in place with the iron.

> **TIP:** *Printing after the pieces are fused in place allows you to place the image exactly where you want it.*

7. Print the "Birds on a Wire" Thermofax screen over the brown fabric with metallic blue paint *(fig. 2)*. Let dry.

> **TIP:** *I heavily handstitched this piece. If you would prefer to machine stitch the work, consider doing that before you add the decay printing in Step 8.*

8. Decay print the white circles using papier mâché lids. Begin with one large circle centered on the runner and then space two smaller circles in the middle of each side *(fig. 3)*. Let dry.

9. Once the table runner is dry, give it a good press and begin adding your stitching. I used straight stitches and X's. This is when you can bring in hints of additional color. Using lighter-weight thread will add to the illusion that it's part of the fabric.

Fig. 1

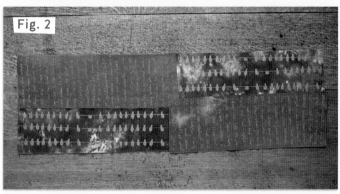

Fig. 2

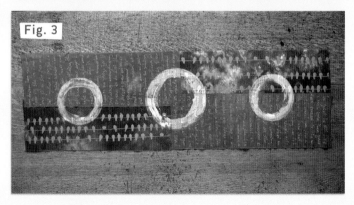

Fig. 3

TIPS: *Begin stitching around the outside of the circles and along the horizontal seams of the two pieces first. This will help hold the rest of the piece in place as you work.*

Allover stitching in tone-on-tone thread adds strength to the work and a subtle texture that complements the printing.

10. Add beads or other embellishments at the edges, if you like. I used a thin hand-sewing needle and beading thread to attach beads to the edges of the table runner. Beading thread is stronger than ordinary sewing thread and won't be cut by any sharp edges on the beads.

FABRIC-WRAPPED CATCHALL BOXES

FINISHED MEASUREMENTS
- One box measures about 4"
  (10 cm) wide × 4" (10 cm) deep × 2"
  (5 cm) tall.

PRINTING TECHNIQUES
- Drop-Cloth Printing (page 64)
- Drawing on Fabric (page 42)

YOU WILL NEED
(FOR ONE BOX)
- Two 4" (10 cm) square papier mâché boxes
- Brown acrylic craft paint
- ¼ yd (23 cm) blue fabric
- Yellow ochre, orange, and white textile paint
- Gelli Arts Gel Printing Plate
- Plastic palette knife and plastic spoons
- Craft glue
- Foam brush
- White acrylic craft paint
- Squeeze bottle with tip

It seems that there are never enough places to wrangle all the bits and baubles that come with everyday life. These handy little boxes are so simple to make and a prime opportunity to show off printed fabric. Make enough to corral all of your odds and ends!

[DESIGN & PRINTING CONSIDERATIONS]

It's difficult to print small pieces of fabric. When making a project with thin strips, print fabric that equals the total amount of the strips. If you need only one small piece, double or triple it until it feels comfortable to handle. Save any leftover bits for future projects.

For small pieces of printed fabric, choose abstract designs. These work best because color becomes the primary focus and jumps out clearly.

Papier mâché boxes can vary slightly from their described size, so it's a good idea to measure them before you cut or tear strips of fabric and adjust the dimensions if necessary. A soft tape measure is great for measuring the length needed for wrapping around the outside and along the inside.

1. Using brown acrylic craft paint and a foam brush, paint two opposite sides of the box and lid on both the outside and inside. Paint about ½" (1.3 cm) in from the edges but leave the center portion of the box and lid unpainted *(fig. 1)*.

> **TIP:** *It's not necessary to paint the entire box because you're going to cover it with a fabric strip. So save the time and the paint!*

2. Print your fabric using the drop-cloth method and the yellow ochre, orange, and white textile paint.

3. Cut or tear fabric into one 3¼" (8.5 cm) wide × 16½" (42 cm) long strip for the box and one 3¼" (8.5 cm) wide × 11½" (29 cm) long strip for the lid *(fig. 2)*.

4. Once the paint on the box is dry, apply some craft glue directly to *one* side of the box and smooth out with a foam brush.

> **TIP:** *Smoothing the glue out with the foam brush will help keep it from bleeding through the fabric.*

Fig. 1

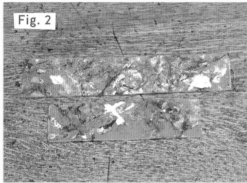

Fig. 2

5. Position the 16½" (42 cm) long piece of fabric over the glue and smooth flat. Do this for each outer surface of the box—around the bottom and back up the other side—applying glue and smoothing the fabric one surface at a time.

> **TIPS:** *Applying the glue one side at a time allows you to work slowly so you can be sure you're positioning your fabric well.*
>
> *Don't be afraid to tug the fabric to get it to stay straight. Cotton stretches and won't mind moving around a little bit.*

6. With the 11½" (29 cm) long strip, repeat the same gluing and fabric application for the lid.

7. Add some white paint to the squeeze bottle and doodle circles on the painted sides of the box and lid to give a little extra detail.

GRANNY'S GARDEN SCARF

FINISHED MEASUREMENTS
- About 10" (25.5 cm) wide × 75" (190.5 cm) long.

PRINTING TECHNIQUES
- Stamping (page 52)

YOU WILL NEED
- 2 yd (1.8 m) each olive and bright green shot cotton
- Self-adhesive foam
- Hexagon template (see page 148)
- Cardboard
- Foam brush
- Gold and white pearlescent or metallic textile paint
- Lana wool/acrylic sewing thread
- Needles for handstitching
- Sewing machine
- Scissors

I may be on the contemporary side of textile art, but I have incredible admiration for traditional quilting. I once saw a Grandmother's Flower Garden quilt at a flea market. It was old and ratty. It had stains, and stitches were missing; where they were managing to hang on, they were loose. It had seen a lot in its little fibery life. I still regret not bringing it home with me and giving it a final place to hang on the wall.

After that encounter, I tried my hand at making a granny's garden quilt but just couldn't take the project to completion. Still wanting to find a way to connect with these beauties, I realized I could mimic the pattern with surface design. I chose to combine it with one of my other addictions—scarves.

[DESIGN & PRINTING CONSIDERATIONS]

The printing on this project is very simple and, as with everything else in this book, that is intentional.

Paint will always add stiffness to your fabric. Textile paint does a great job of minimizing the effect because of the way it's formulated but when you are printing a wearable project, you need to be careful how heavily you paint it so you don't create armor. By using a bold graphic image that spans the width of the scarf, you can get away with less detailed printing while still maintaining good drape on the final product.

I wanted a clean repeat of the Grandmother's Flower Garden pattern, so I designed the stamp in a way that would allow me to easily do that. Creating a stamp with self-adhesive foam is perfect for this project because we are able to customize it to our exact needs.

I'm a cotton girl through and through. Silk and lightweight linen are wonderful for scarves, but I was determined to find a cotton that would work. Shot cottons fit the bill. They're very lightweight (meaning considerably thinner than the Kona cotton we've been using elsewhere), and they have incredible depth because they're woven with two different colored threads. In fact, some of them have a kind of iridescence that appears to shift with the light.

As a nod to my love of antique quilts, I chose colors that are darker in appearance to imply patina. But I didn't want it to be boring, so I used a bright green for the back of the scarf (also shot cotton). When the scarf is wrapped around your neck, you'll get a lovely mix of dark tones and bright pops.

I wanted to honor that little quilt I saw with its missing and disrupted stitches, so only some of the hexagons around the stamps are stitched. I stitched this project using Aurifil's Lana thread, which is 50% acrylic and 50% wool. It has a homey feeling and complements the goal of the scarf perfectly.

I did not fuse these layers together, opting to just pin it really well before stitching, since I wanted to keep it as fluid as possible. Mistyfuse is an excellent option if you prefer to fuse, as it will not change the hand at all.

1. Cut or tear one 11" (28 cm) wide × 72" (183 cm) long piece of shot cotton fabric in each color.

2. Using the template, trace seven 1¼" (3.2 cm) hexagons onto self-adhesive foam and cut out *(fig. 1)*.

3. Cut a piece of cardboard 11" (28 cm) wide × 9" (23 cm) long.

4. Arrange the hexagons in a Grandmother's Flower Garden pattern onto the center of the cardboard.

5. With a foam brush, paint white iridescent paint on the center hexagon and gold on the "petal" hexagons *(fig. 2)*. Stamp flower along the length of the entire scarf, lining up the edge of the last stamped image with the edge of the cardboard. This will ensure even spacing along the entire length and will allow you to stamp a total of nine flowers *(fig. 3)*. Let dry.

6. Pin the two pieces of fabric with right sides together. Machine stitch along the 72" (183 cm) sides only.

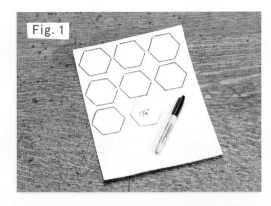

Fig. 1

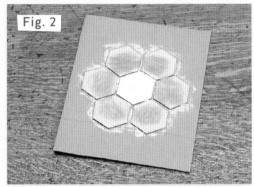

Fig. 2

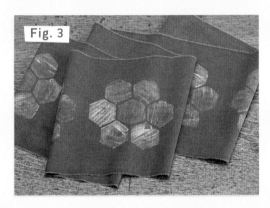

Fig. 3

TIP: *I left the short ends of the scarf as raw edges to help carry through my homage to the little tattered quilt I saw. If you prefer a cleaner edge, sew along these edges as well, but leave yourself a large enough opening along the seam to turn the scarf right side out.*

7. Turn the scarf right side out and press along the 72" (183 cm) sides to get a crisp flat seam.

8. Handstitch rows of straight stitches through both layers along the long edges and in random locations around the hexagons.

FINISHED MEASUREMENTS

○ Each tile shown at left measures 6"
(15 cm) square.

PRINTING TECHNIQUES

○ Stamping (page 52)

○ Shadow Printing (page 74)

○ Thermofax Screen Printing
(page 68)

○ Decay Printing (page 56)

**YOU WILL NEED
(FOR ONE SET OF TILES)**

○ Three 6" (15 cm) square pre-
stretched canvases

○ ¼ yd (23 cm) brown fabric

○ Metallic olive green, pearl
turquoise, and white textile paint

○ 4 precut foam football shapes
(about 1¼" [3.2 cm] wide each)

*Note: If you can't find foam foot-
ball shapes, use the template on
page 148 and cut the shape out of
self-adhesive foam.*

○ 3" × 6" (7.5 × 15 cm) piece
of cardboard

○ Foam brushes

○ "Cascading Branches" Thermofax
screen (see Resources)

○ 5" (12.5 cm) round papier mâché lid

○ Craft glue and paintbrush

○ Dark brown acrylic craft paint and
paintbrush

○ Screw eyes and picture wire
or sawtooth hangers

I'm a huge fan of ceramic tiles, particularly ones that come in sets of two and three with the imagery continuing between them. It's easy to mimic this type of effect with printed fabric. This is a no-stitch project that relies on what we learned in the layered printing chapter (page 92).

I call these little works of art "fabric tiles," and they hang easily on my walls next to their ceramic cousins.

DESIGN & PRINTING CONSIDERATIONS

Always print the fabric as a single piece for this kind of project. This eliminates any need to line things up later.

In order to create a strong connection between each tile, make sure there is an element that is bold and runs across the entire composition.

Depending on the size of the canvas you want to use, adjust the size of your imagery accordingly. We used smaller images for our project because of the petite canvas. But if you want to create a very large set, be bold and go big!

1. Cut or tear a 6" × 18" (15 × 45.5 cm) piece of brown fabric. (No seam allowances are needed.)

2. Create your foam stamp using precut football shapes or shape cut from template (*fig. 1*).

3. Lightly mark the fabric piece at 6" (15 cm) and 12" (30.5 cm). Shadow print with the stamp and metallic olive green paint. Print the first pass of the shadow printing across the entire strip, the second pass up to the 12" (30.5 cm) mark, and the final pass up to the 6" (15 cm) mark (*fig. 2*). Let dry.

TIP: *This printing is meant to be subtle because the intent is to create a serene abstract piece. If you want an effect that is more energetic, use a color that has more contrast with the base fabric.*

4. Print the second layer across the entire top of the strip using the Thermofax screen print and white paint (*fig. 3*). Let dry.

5. Using a 5" (12.5 cm) round papier mâché lid, print a circle using pearl turquoise paint at the 6" (15 cm) and 12" (30.5 cm) marks. Line up the middle of the circle so that it is centered at these points, but don't stress if it's not perfectly centered. After those two circles are printed, print half circles at each end (*fig. 4*). Let dry.

6. Cut a slit at the 6" (15 cm) mark and 12" (30.5 cm) mark. Cut or tear the fabric into three pieces.

7. Squirt a small amount of craft glue on the canvas and quickly spread it across the entire canvas with the paintbrush. Make sure it's a thin layer; you just want to hold the fabric down, not saturate it with glue.

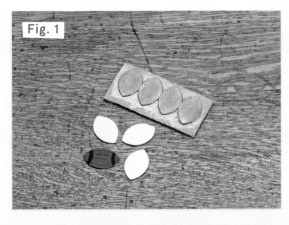

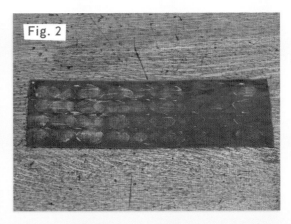

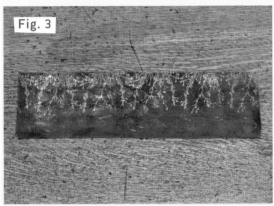

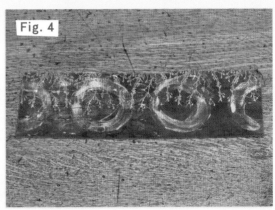

TIP: You may find that tearing the fabric distorts it a little bit so that it's not a perfect 6" (15 cm) square. If this happens on one of the end squares, position it so that the extra fabric wraps around the outside edge of the canvas. If it happens on the center square of fabric, center it and let it wrap evenly around the edges.

8. Paint the edges of your tile with acrylic craft paint. Let the paint travel up slightly onto the fabric to seal any edges the glue didn't catch and create an integrated "frame" to the piece.

TIP: At this point you may want to add a small touch to each piece. Small details will help add unity to the work, but you don't want to detract from the composition. I added two faint orange circles on the corners of the end pieces and connected them with a single line of black paint across all three tiles.

9. Add wire or sawtooth hangers and hang up on the wall!

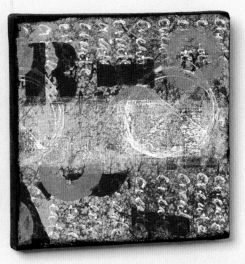

These fabric tiles were so much fun to create, I decided to make two more sets using the same construction techniques but different printed designs. As you can see, two larger tiles can also form a strong piece of wall art. Each tile in the alternative triptych measures 5" (12.5 cm) square. Each tile in the pair of tiles measures 8" (20.5 cm).

MEDITATION CLOTH

FINISHED MEASUREMENTS
- Meditation cloth measures about 7" (18 cm) wide × 12" (30.5 cm) long. Optional display board measures 9" (23 cm) wide × 16" (40.5 cm) long.

PRINTING TECHNIQUES
- Color-Wash Printing (page 38)
- Decay Printing (page 56)
- Drawing on Fabric (page 42)

YOU WILL NEED
- ½ yd (23 cm) white or other light neutral fabric
- Machine-weight sewing thread and handstitching needle
- Gold yellow, olive, brown, and white textile paint
- Letter stencil
- Rubber brayer
- Squeeze bottles with tips

Optional display board:
- 16½" (42 cm) long × 9" (23 cm) wide piece of cardboard
- Mistyfuse
- Iron
- 16½" (42 cm) long × 10" (25.5 cm) wide piece of light brown fabric
- Two 2" (5 cm) square pieces of felt
- Two 1" (2.5 cm) buttons
- Pearl cotton thread
- Craft glue
- Clothespin

Sometimes we need a project that forces us to slow down, unplug, and reconnect with ourselves. Meditation cloth does just that.

I've been making these bits of fabric for years. They vary depending on what I'm experimenting with in my textile art at the time and almost always get chopped up for use in another project. But lately I've come to appreciate them for what they are and have been leaving them whole.

This is the type of project that you stash in your purse and work on here and there. It's not meant to be completed in one running swoop but rather to be a way to pass those idle moments or to still your mind during a stressful day.

[DESIGN & PRINTING CONSIDERATIONS]

This project focuses on handstitching and the meditative qualities it possesses. If you are unable to stitch by hand or simply have an undying affection for your sewing machine, don't think you should skip this one. I encourage you to try handstitching, but if it's not your thing, by all means work with your machine.

Meditation cloth is about simplicity. The printing will be simple, and we'll have large portions of unprinted fabric. The lesson is to learn to embrace the pauses we have in our lives, and this is reflected in the large breaks in printing.

I'm going to walk you through how to create a small piece, but there is no limit to how large these can be. Larger pieces can be used as wall display pieces or table coverings. Smaller pieces are wonderful additions to corkboards or cubicle walls. This is one of those things that you make just because you can, even though you don't really have an end purpose for it. I display mine on a little board made from recycled shipping box cardboard, leaning it against the wall on my desk. I've provided instructions for how to make one.

1. Cut or tear fabric into three 2½" (6.5 cm) wide × 12" (30.5 cm) long pieces. (No seam allowances are needed.)

2. Overlap the pieces along the long edges with a ¼" (6 mm) seam allowance and stitch along the seams to attach them into a single piece of fabric that measures about 7" (18 cm) wide × 12" (30.5 cm) long (fig. 1).

3. Stitch a random plus-sign pattern (see page 88) down the center strip of the fabric (fig. 2).

4. Using a brayer and gold yellow paint, color-wash print a 5" (12.5 cm) section on one end of the cloth (fig. 3). Let dry.

5. Using a letter stencil and olive paint, stencil a single letter repeatedly along the center strip (fig. 4), printing the letter both right-reading and backward to form a design. Let dry.

> **TIP:** *I like to use letters and text as a way to add shape and movement to a piece, not always to convey a word. Flipping the letter while printing reduces it to a shape. Use whatever letter appeals to you the most, or print a word, if you'd prefer.*

6. Using brown paint in a squeeze bottle, draw five rows of plus signs in the top of the gold color-wash area. Let dry.

7. Using white paint in a squeeze bottle, draw dots along the entire length of the long edges and in between the plus signs.

OPTIONAL DISPLAY BOARD

1. Lay Mistyfuse across the cardboard.

2. Gently lay the 16½" (42 cm) long × 10" (25.5 cm) wide piece of fabric over top of the Mistyfuse and cardboard, leaving about ½" (1.3 cm) overhang of fabric on the long sides. Fuse the fabric in place with the iron.

3. Flip the cardboard over and run a line of glue along the edge of the fabric. Fold it over, and press the fabric against the cardboard.

4. Sew a 1" (2.5 cm) diameter button to the center of each felt square with a long piece of pearl cotton extending between the two of them like a clothesline.

> **TIP:** *How much slack you leave in your line is up to you. I left about a 7" (18 cm) length between the buttons.*

5. Glue the felt squares down to the top corners of the board. Let dry.

6. Clip your meditation cloth to the line with a clothespin and proudly display.

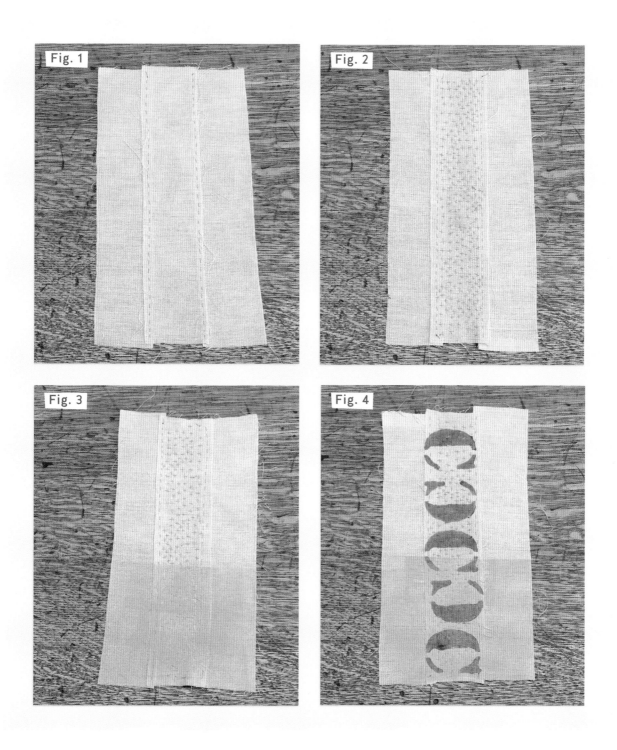

PETITE STACKED COLLAGES

FINISHED MEASUREMENTS

- The collages shown at left measure from about 3" (7.5 cm) square to about 4½" (11.5 cm) square, but you can make them any size you wish.

YOU WILL NEED (FOR SEVERAL COLLAGES)

- Scraps of printed and unprinted fabric
- Felt
- Buttons in various sizes
- Embroidery floss or thread and needles
- Soho Fabric Glue (optional)

Even if you're being very deliberate about how you print fabric, it's inevitable that you will have leftover scraps of fabric or even fabric from projects that just didn't work out the way you wanted. It's all part of the process, so instead of making plans to bury them in the backyard, use these bits to your advantage.

Petite stacked collages are my answer to what to do with these little cast-offs. I use almost all my leftovers to make these little gems, and I think you'll agree, they're quite fun.

These mini collages are also the perfect portable project. I make up a plastic baggie with fabric, thread, felt, and any other item needed and leave it in my purse.

DESIGN & PRINTING CONSIDERATIONS

Because we're using fabric that is left over or that went astray in the design process, we're dealing with a hodgepodge of colors and imagery. These little fellows are a great lesson in the importance of having a focal point. You can break up the busyness of the fabric by using scraps of unprinted fabric and create a focal point with a single element, such as a button or large embellishment.

Avoid adding lots of little embellishments, as that will push these over the edge into chaotic design. While I love a frantically energetic composition, these little pieces don't bear that kind of look very well. Since our goal is to use these leftover pieces to our advantage, we need to dial it back and try not to return them to the unwanted pile.

These little guys look great framed. Decide what size frame you want to use and then make the piece to fit the opening. In other words, put the cart before the horse if you want to display these. It sounds like a "Duh!" thing to say, but you'd be surprised how many times I've made the mistake of creating the work and then scrambling to find a display method.

These are great additions to future artwork, as little gifts to a fiber-loving friend, or to trade like artist trading cards.

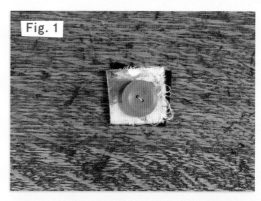

Fig. 1

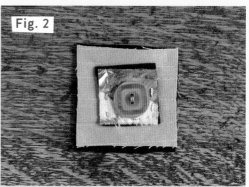

Fig. 2

Fig. 3

1. We are going to make these in reverse order, starting with the top layer. This is the layer in which you will want to display the most interesting fabric so that it shows the most. Hold the button over the fabric and freehand cut a square for it to sit on. Cut felt to the same size as the fabric. (I used leftover fabric from the Fabric-Wrapped Catchall Boxes project, page 120.)

TIP: *You can cut the felt a little bit larger to create an extra peek of color.*

2. Stitch the button down through the fabric and felt (*fig. 1*).

3. Use a solid piece of fabric for the middle piece. (I used leftover unprinted fabric from the Coffee Talk Hoops project, page 112.) Hold the stitched top piece with the button over top of the fabric and cut around it, leaving about a ½" (1.3 cm) border around each side or however much you would like to see. Cut a piece of felt to the same size.

4. Stitch the top piece down to the middle piece and the felt using the embroidery stitch of your choice *(fig. 2)*. I used a straight stitch (page 85).

5. Create the base of your collage by laying the stitched top/middle piece over top of more printed fabric and cut to the size that makes you happy. Cut a piece of felt to the same size.

TIP: *For the base of my collage, I used the fabric left over from my first attempt at designing the Reclaimed Intentions Banner project (page 142). It allowed me to still use all my hard work, but by putting it on the bottom, the bits that I wasn't so happy with don't show.*

6. Stitch the top/middle piece to the base and the felt using the stitch of your choice.

TIP: *Since we have some pretty conflicting colors in this piece, I eased the transition between the neutral fabric and the dark pink base by using a duller orange thread. This creates a bridge between the bright orange button and the dark background.*

7. If you use an already-stitched piece for any of your layers (like I did for the bottom layer), run a very thin bead of fabric glue around the edges of the fabric and press to the felt *(fig. 3)*. This will help prevent any stitches you may have cut through from pulling out.

And that's it! You've got a cute little collage ready to be incorporated into future projects, and all your hard work from printing other projects gets put to use! Win-win!

strive · love · peace · kindness · harmony · no
judgement · creation · laugh · inspire · embrace

smile · be kind · happiness · give · write
poetry · daydream · allow failure · hug your

dog · sing loudly · be bold · challenge
everything · dance badly · paint with abandon ·

never stop trying · keep an open mind ·
don't fit in · make each day count · imagine ·

let life evolve · make art · learn · make
mistakes · compassion · live life fully ·

RECLAIMED INTENTIONS BANNER

FINISHED MEASUREMENTS

- Banner measures about 13" (33 cm) wide × 27½" (70 cm) long. Board measures about 16" (40.5 cm) wide × 38" (96.5 cm) tall.

PRINTING TECHNIQUES

- Any technique(s) from Fabric-Printing Techniques (page 36)
- Color-Wash Printing (page 38)
- Drawing on Fabric (page 42)

YOU WILL NEED

- 10 strips of fabric 6" (15 cm) wide × 13" (33 cm) long in colors of your choice (no seam allowances needed)
- Paints and printing tools of your choice
- 27" (68.5 cm) long × 12½" (31.5 cm) wide piece of batting (optional)
- 27" (68.5 cm) long × 12½" (31.5 cm) wide piece of cotton fabric for backing
- Mistyfuse and iron
- White paint
- 2" (5 cm) wide rubber brayer
- Soho Fabric Glue
- Black textile paint
- Squeeze bottle with tip
- Sewing machine
- Hand-embroidery needles and thread
- Embellishments (optional)

This project began life as a flag bunting that just didn't grow into what I had envisioned. I have two philosophies when it comes to projects: (1) if it's fighting me and I can't bring it to a point that feels organically complete, it's not meant to be, and (2) everything can be repurposed. This banner embodies these two ideas. The original project was meant to capture positive ideas and intentions. That part remained, but the fabric was rearranged into strips, mimicking reclaimed wood art. It's a reminder of the things I hold dear and a commitment to always use all the fabric I print.

[DESIGN & PRINTING CONSIDERATIONS]

Never be afraid to dump a project and start a new design. If you continue to hit a wall when you're designing a piece, don't waste your energy trying to force it into something it doesn't want to be. Instead, set it aside and imagine what it could be if it was entirely different; let the enthusiasm that comes with a new idea carry it into a new state.

When you repurpose fabric from another project, additional printing is often needed to make the new concept gel. This can make the project pretty stiff and not always the easiest to hand-stitch. If this happens, put it under the machine.

I loved the idea of this being a reclaimed project so much that I took it a step further with my display method. A friend of mine built a display of reclaimed wood from old fencing for me, and I nailed the completed project to it. If you don't want to go this far, this project will look equally nice attached to a pre-stretched painted canvas or hung against a wall by means of a hanging sleeve on the back. Be creative! Mixing materials when it comes to the display method can really take a project from ho-hum to something unique and interesting.

1. Print the pieces of fabric using any printing process you've learned in the book. After printing, tear each piece into two 3" (7.5 cm) wide by 13" (33 cm) long pieces. You will use only one of each in the project, so keep the leftovers for a future project.

TIP: Larger pieces of fabric are easier to print than skinny pieces. Plus, by printing a little bit extra, you'll have pieces of fabric that you love ready to quickly make into a new project. This is not the same as randomly printing. Printing extra pieces this way ensures that you build a small collection of printed fabric that you love and will use, as opposed to just printing with abandon and hoping you end up with something you love.

2. Lay the Mistyfuse over the backing fabric.

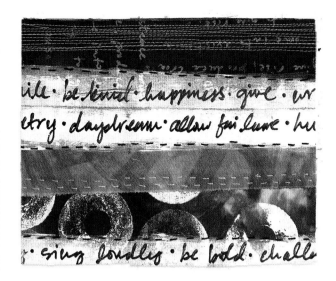

TIP: The way I constructed this project is by fusing the fabric strips directly to the backing fabric. There is no middle layer as in quilting. If you would like to make your piece more quilt like, lay the Mistyfuse in Step 2 over batting.

3. Lay the strips over top of the Mistyfuse, overlapping the edges so they fit on the backing. The overlap doesn't need to be consistent, just make sure the Mistyfuse and backing fabric aren't showing.

4. Fuse the strips into place with the iron.

5. Color-wash print every other overlap seam using the rubber brayer and white paint. Start with the first seam at the top of the banner and then skip to every other seam. You will want to print over the same seams two or three times to create a strong white band *(fig. 1)*. Let it dry in between each printing.

6. Once the color-wash strips are dry, glue down the seams that run through the center of them since we won't be stitching them. *Don't* glue the other seams; glue only the ones that *are* color-wash printed.

7. Using black paint in a bottle, write sentiments or thoughts you find encouraging. This time the words are front and center, so add text that you don't mind other people reading.

Fig. 1

POSITIVE INTENTIONS

Need some ideas for what to write on your banner? Here's what I wrote on mine:

- ★ strive
- ★ love
- ★ peace
- ★ kindness
- ★ harmony
- ★ no judgment
- ★ creation
- ★ laugh
- ★ inspire
- ★ embrace
- ★ smile
- ★ be kind
- ★ happiness
- ★ give
- ★ write poetry
- ★ daydream
- ★ allow failure
- ★ hug your dog

- ★ sing loudly
- ★ be bold
- ★ challenge everything
- ★ dance badly
- ★ paint with abandon
- ★ never stop trying
- ★ keep an open mind
- ★ don't fit in
- ★ make every day count
- ★ imagine
- ★ let life evolve
- ★ make art
- ★ learn
- ★ make mistakes
- ★ compassion
- ★ live life fully

TIP: *If you added batting to your project, you'll need to add backing fabric to your project before heading on to Step 8. You could fuse the backing layer to the batting using Mistyfuse or just pin it in place until you've finished stitching.*

8. Add stitching and any embellishments that strike your fancy.

TIPS: *Mix up the types of stitching. I handstitched with various weights of handstitching thread combined with some rows of machine stitching.*

Let all the knots and thread tails hang out; let them do what they naturally want to do!

Some areas of this project can be difficult to stitch through, so you may prefer to use only the machine.

9. Attach the project to your chosen display method.

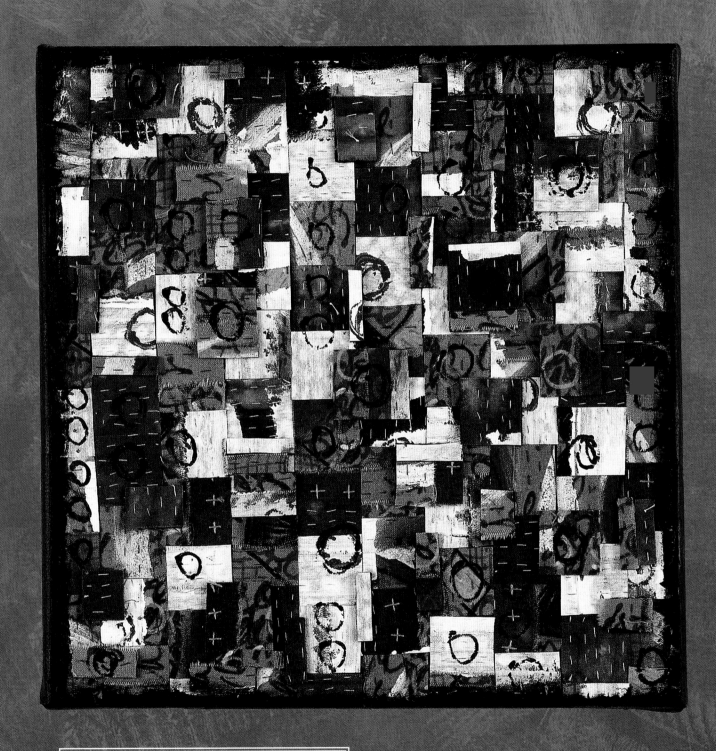

Remnants Collage 35. 10" × 10" (25.5 × 25.5 cm);
fused appliqué, handstitching; handprinted and
hand-dyed fabrics, canvas.

INTENTIONAL PRINTING IN ACTION

Lynn Krawczyk

"

My relationship with fabric has moved and shifted over the years. I'm at a place now in which I feel fully connected with it, and as a result, I find myself more willing to push what I can do with it. I find my stitched projects less precious, viewing them more as a gateway to more possibilities should the idea strike.

This piece, *Remnants Collage 35*, is part of an ongoing series of works that have gone under the rotary cutter to be reinvented. This collage started out as a simpler composition that consisted of torn strips of the original printed fabric fused down to a piece of felt alongside a solid blue piece of fabric.

I wasn't unhappy with it at that stage, but I kept staring at all those colors and swoops of shapes and wanted to reduce them to their most basic elements. I took my rotary cutter and cut the entire stitched piece into 1" (2.5 cm) squares. Then I arranged them in a random mosaic on canvas, placing some pieces on top to create a stacked appearance. The resulting piece is perfect to me, a true representation of color in its most honest form.

"

— *Lynn Krawczyk*

Printing techniques: Drawing on fabric (page 42), shadow printing (page 74), decay printing with papier mâché lids (page 56).

TEMPLATES

Photocopying allowed

Beanbag Desk Weights (page 108); photocopy at 200%

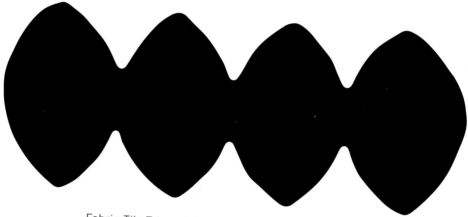

Fabric-Tile Triptych (page 128); photocopy at 100%

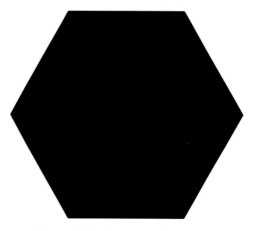

Granny's Garden Scarf (page 124);
photocopy at 100%

Photocopying allowed

Coffee Talk Hoops (page 112);
photocopy at 100%

ACKNOWLEDGMENTS

I went into writing a book thinking it would be like writing a giant magazine article. Along the way, I have come to realize that each book that is ever created is an incredible orchestra of moving parts and talented individuals. I am eternally grateful to the following people for helping me create this book:

My editor, Michelle Bredeson, who helped me stay on track (calmly) through the entire process, and all the talented individuals at Interweave. It's truly a joy to work with everyone there.

My mentor and friend, Lesley Riley, for all of her wisdom and guidance.

The contributing artists featured in the book who added a unique perspective that I treasure so much.

My friends who listened to me go on and on about writing and printing fabric with great patience and interest.

The surface-design community that continues to print fabric, fling paint, and make amazing art every single day. I'm grateful to be counted among you.

RESOURCES

PRINTING SUPPLIES

Squeeze bottles, foam brushes, adhesive foam
Dick Blick Art Materials
PO Box 1267
Galesburg, IL 61402
(800) 828-4548
dickblick.com

Gelli Arts Printing Plate
Gelli Arts
810 S. 8th St.
Philadelphia, PA 19147
(800) 580-4198
gelliarts.com

Neopaque, Lumiere, Textile Color, and Dye-Na-Flow paints
Jacquard Products
Rupert, Gibbon & Spider, Inc.
PO Box 425
Healdsburg, CA 95448
(800) 442-0455
jacquardproducts.com

Mistyfuse fusible web
Mistyfuse
(631) 750-8500
mistyfuse.com

Simply Screen Paint
Plaid Enterprises
(800) 842-4197
simplyscreenonline.com

Kona cotton fabric
Robert Kaufman Fabrics
Box 59266
Greenmead Station
Los Angeles, CA 90059
(800) 877-2066
robertkaufman.com

Thermofax screens
Smudged Textiles Shop
etsy.com/shop/SmudgedTextilesShop

BOOKS AND DVDS

Anderson, Frieda L. *Fabric to Dye For: Create 72 Hand-Dyed Colors for Your Stash.* Concord, CA: C&T Publishing, 2010.

Dunnewold, Jane. *Art Cloth: A Guide to Surface Design for Fabric.* Loveland, CO: Interweave, 2010.

Flint, India. *Eco Colour: Botanical Dyes for Beautiful Textiles.* Loveland, CO: Interweave, 2010.

Johnston, Ann. *Color by Accident: Low-Water Immersion Dyeing.* Self-published, 1997.

Krawczyk, Lynn. *Color Theory Made Easy: An Exploration of Color & Composition through Surface Design* (DVD). Loveland, CO: Interweave, 2013.

Krawczyk, Lynn. *Print, Design, Compose: From Surface Design to Fabric Art* (DVD). Loveland, CO: Interweave, 2011.

INDEX

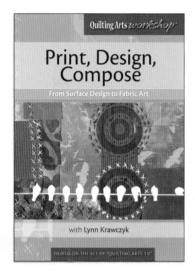
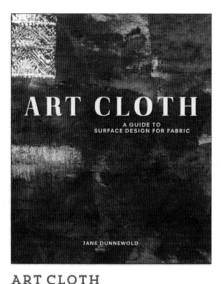
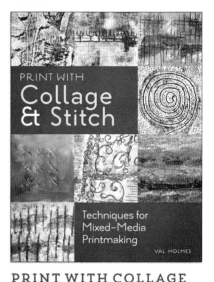